Bringing good food and families together for 75 years.

THE KRAFT COOKBOOK

BY
THE KRAFT KITCHENS

The Benjamin Company/Rutledge Books

Contents

Introduction

The year 1978 marks the seventy-fifth anniversary of the beginning, by J. L. Kraft, of a business to which he gave his name and devoted his life. The organization which now bears the Kraft name is known throughout the world for quality food products. For more than fifty of these years, the Kraft Kitchens have enjoyed a close association with consumers, providing recipes and food ideas to enhance daily menus. It is, therefore, with great pride and pleasure that we present this anniversary collection of recipes.

In this collection, you will find treasured classics, popular television recipes, and some recent favorites. Many of the classics have been in our files for almost a half-century. Through the years, the criteria for Kraft recipes have not changed. Our recipes must be practical, economical, nutritious, and imaginative. They must also respond to the needs and interests of our consumers. We think cooking should be a creative experience as well as an everyday necessity.

The skills and talents of hundreds of people from many departments are represented in this book—especially the efforts of the Kraft Kitchens and Photography Department.

We hope that these recipes will add to your culinary enjoyment and that you will join us in celebrating our long tradition of "good food and good food ideas."

The Kraft Story

1903–1915

In 1903, James Lewis Kraft (known as "J. L.") came to Chicago from Ft. Erie, Ontario, Canada. His assets were $65.00 in cash, a knowledge of food and marketing, the ability to work hard, and a determination to build a quality cheese business—one that was destined to become worldwide.

J. L.'s $65.00 paid for one month's lodging and breakfast rolls, a horse named Paddy, and a small stock of cheese. With courage and perseverance—and the help of Paddy, whom he referred to as his original partner—J. L. established a brisk business. In 1904, J. L. wrote to a friend describing the business: "It is simply a grocery route on a large scale. You take a horse and wagon and get customers that you can call on once or twice a week and supply them regularly. I am driving one wagon myself, and am taking care of the horses myself, but if all goes well I think I will have four horses by Christmas."

By 1905, the expanding business was moved to larger quarters and two years later J. L. asked four brothers—Fred, Charles, Norman, and John—to join him. At the first stockholders meeting in 1909, the Kraft Company became the J. L. Kraft and Bros. Co.

Considering the methods of cheesemaking and curing known in those days, nationwide distribution was difficult, but J. L. and his associates extended their operations to major cities in the East in 1912, and also began importing fine cheeses from Europe.

J. L. soon realized another of his original ambitions—to develop a process for marketing his highly perishable products in convenient packages, with good keeping quality, no waste, and uniform flavor and texture. For centuries, this goal had eluded cheesemakers both here and abroad. Working with a double boiler and a copper kettle, he researched one method after another until he perfected a formula that would meet consumer expectations for a cheese product of uniform quality that would keep better and cook better. The new product is now known as process cheese. In 1915, Kraft introduced cheese in 3½-ounce and 7¾-ounce tins, marking one of the greatest advances in all cheese-making history. Its popularity was so great that new production facilities were added to handle the demand. Today process cheese products are marketed throughout the world.

Appetizers

Appetizers have been an American tradition since the colonial era when entertaining, among the aristocrats, was always an elegant and lavish occasion. Originally, "hors d'oeuvres" were served as a separate course before dinner to whet the appetite and were limited to dainty canapés, caviar, pâtés, seafood bisques, consommés, sorbets, and aperitifs.

Today, the variety of appetizers served in the American home is almost unlimited. They may be hot or cold, simple or fancy, light or hearty. They are served for many social occasions, casual or formal — to introduce dinner, for evening entertaining, as a complete buffet meal, or at receptions and banquets. Best of all, almost any food — fruits, vegetables, meats, cheese, small salads, relishes — is acceptable appetizer fare.

There are few rules to inhibit creative appetizer cookery. The food, however, should suit the occasion. For example, serve: small portions of one or two light foods before dinner; a wide selection of dishes for a complete appetizer meal; hot appetizers in winter and cold in summer; and a few do-ahead specialties for late evening entertaining. "Prepare in advance" is always a good rule since a gracious host or hostess should attend the guests, not the food, once the party begins.

The following recipes are a few Kraft favorites that have been accumulating since the early 1920s. Dips, spreads, cheese balls, fondues, and many more — whatever your pleasure!

Hot Crabmeat Appetizer

A truly elegant Kraft "classic," this flavorful baked appetizer is the center of attention at any party.

1 8-oz. pkg. Philadelphia
   Brand cream cheese
1½ cups (7½-oz. can)
   flaked drained
   crabmeat
2 tablespoons finely
   chopped onion

2 tablespoons milk
½ teaspoon cream style
   horseradish
¼ teaspoon salt
   Dash of pepper
⅓ cup sliced almonds,
   toasted

Combine softened cream cheese, crabmeat, onion, milk, horseradish and seasonings, mixing until well blended. Spoon into 9-inch pie plate or oven-proof dish; sprinkle with nuts. Bake at 375°, 15 minutes. Serve as a dip or spread with crackers, chips or raw vegetables.

Variation: An 8-oz. can of clams and a sprinkle of dill are excellent alternatives for the crabmeat and almonds.

Clam Appetizer Dip

A Kraft original and a favorite for entertaining.

1 8-oz. can minced clams
1 garlic clove, cut in half
1 8-oz. pkg. Philadelphia
   Brand cream cheese
2 teaspoons lemon juice

1½ teaspoons
   Worcestershire
   sauce
½ teaspoon salt
   Dash of pepper

Drain clams, reserving ¼ cup liquid. Rub inside of mixing bowl with garlic. Combine clams, clam liquid, softened cream cheese and remaining ingredients, mixing until well blended. Chill. Serve with chips. 1⅔ cups

Clam Appetizer Dip was one of the first recipes demonstrated on television. A few days later the entire stock of canned clams on the Atlantic seaboard had been sold out. East coast packers requested that Kraft alert them in advance whenever the recipe was to be shown again.

Aristocrat Dip

A Kraft "classic" in the best tradition, perfect either as an epicurean dip for entertaining or as an elegant dressing for crisp lettuce wedges or slices of tomato.

1 cup Kraft real
  mayonnaise
½ cup dairy sour cream
¼ cup chopped parsley
2 tablespoons chopped
  onion

1 tablespoon anchovy
  paste
1 garlic clove, minced
Dash of pepper

Combine ingredients; mix well. Chill. Serve with shrimp, raw cauliflowerets, zucchini sticks or mushroom caps. 1¾ cups

Curry Dip

Centered on a platter of assorted vegetables—cucumber slices, cherry tomatoes, mushroom caps, carrot sticks, Belgian endive—this is a lovely appetizer for a party.

1 cup Kraft real
  mayonnaise
½ cup dairy sour cream

2 tablespoons green
  onion slices
1 teaspoon curry powder

Combine ingredients; mix well. Serve with chips or fresh vegetable dippers. 1½ cups

This dip recipe—a frequent favorite on Kraft television commercials—can be doubled or tripled as needed to feed a crowd.

Potted Cheese

An imaginative (and economical) use of any firm leftover cheese. Most cheese flavors are compatible—Swiss, monterey jack, muenster, brick, caraway or edam.

1 cup (4 ozs.) shredded
  Cracker Barrel sharp
  cheddar cheese
1 cup (4 ozs.) shredded
  Casino muenster cheese

2 tablespoons soft
  margarine
2 tablespoons port
¼ teaspoon paprika

Combine all ingredients, beating until smooth and well blended. Chill. Serve as a spread for crackers, melba toast and rye or pumpernickel bread. 1 cup

"Philly" Avocado Dip

Thanks to cream cheese, this adaptation of the Mexican favorite, guacamole, is extra creamy and flavorful.

1 8-oz. pkg. Philadelphia
  Brand cream cheese
2 medium avocados,
  peeled, mashed
1 tablespoon lemon juice

1 tablespoon finely
  chopped onion
½ teaspoon salt
  Dash of Worcestershire
  sauce

Combine softened cream cheese and avocado, mixing until well blended. Add remaining ingredients; mix well. Serve with corn or tortilla chips and vegetable dippers. 2 cups

In 1914, the first Kraft cheese factory was established in Stockton, Illinois. One of the Kraft brothers, Norman, went to Stockton with his bride to run the plant.

Swiss Cheese Fondue

Particularly suited to winter entertaining, this appetizer fondue also can be served as a main course.

1 8-oz. pkg. Kraft Swiss
  cheese slices, cut into
  strips
1 tablespoon flour
1 garlic clove, cut in half

1 cup dry white wine
2 tablespoons kirsch
  Dash of nutmeg
  Salt and pepper

Toss cheese with flour. Rub inside of fondue pot or electric skillet with garlic. Add wine; heat until bubbles rise to surface. Do not boil. Add ½ cup cheese mixture; stir constantly until melted. Repeat until all cheese has been added. Stir in kirsch and seasonings. Keep fondue bubbling while serving. Dip chunks of bread into fondue. If fondue becomes too thick, add small amount of wine. 3 to 4 servings

For the Swiss, fondues evoke pleasant memories of camaraderie and romance. The trick to fondue is melting the cheese thoroughly without boiling. Traditionally, fondues are served in earthenware pots, but any container in which the cheese mixture can be kept bubbling hot works well.

"Philly" Avocado Dip→

Epicure's Edam

Smooth but fluffy, this spread owes its great flavor to a perfect marriage of edam with sherry.

1 26-oz. Kraft edam cheese	¼ cup soft margarine
	3 tablespoons sherry

Slice top from cheese. Remove cheese from center, leaving ½-inch shell. Shred cheese; add margarine and sherry, beating until smooth and well blended. Refill shell; chill. Serve with crackers.

To prevent the wax coating from cracking, the cheese should be at room temperature before cutting.

Cheery Cheddar Spread

An armchair sportsman's specialty—just stretch out with your favorite beverage, a box of crackers, and this robust cheese spread.

2 cups (8 ozs.) shredded Kraft sharp cheddar cheese	Dash of cayenne
	1 tablespoon chopped chives
¼ cup beer	2 teaspoons chopped pimiento
2 tablespoons margarine	
½ teaspoon prepared mustard	

Combine cheese, beer, margarine, mustard and cayenne, beating until smooth and well blended. Stir in chives and pimiento. Serve with party rye bread and pretzels. 1¾ cups

Mock Pâté

A firmly established favorite that appeals to all ages.

1 8-oz. pkg. Philadelphia Brand cream cheese	1 teaspoon lemon juice
1 8-oz. pkg. liver sausage	1 teaspoon Worcestershire sauce
1 tablespoon chopped onion	Dash of salt and pepper

Combine softened cream cheese and liver sausage, mixing until well blended. Add remaining ingredients; mix well. Chill. Serve with party rye or pumpernickel bread or assorted crackers. 2 cups

Country Club Appetizer Mold

A decorative appetizer for buffet service, this frosted egg salad mold can be prepared in advance and refrigerated until party time.

10 hard-cooked eggs,
finely chopped
⅓ cup Kraft real
mayonnaise
¼ cup green onion slices
½ teaspoon salt
½ teaspoon dill weed

Dash of pepper
* * *
1 3-oz. pkg. cream cheese
3 tablespoons Kraft real
mayonnaise
1 tablespoon chopped
pitted ripe olives

Combine eggs, mayonnaise, onions and seasonings; mix well. Press firmly into 3-cup bowl. Chill several hours or overnight. Unmold on serving plate.

Combine softened cream cheese and mayonnaise, mixing until well blended. Spread over mold. Chill. Top with olives. Serve with party pumpernickel or rye bread. Approximately 3 cups

To protect the cream cheese frosting, cover the mold with a large bowl before refrigerating.

Tropical Cheese Log

A sophisticated spread that is a pleasing combination of such unlikely ingredients as cheddar cheese, dried apricots and ginger. Make ahead—it will keep for several days in the refrigerator.

1 8-oz. pkg. Philadelphia
Brand cream cheese
1 8¼-oz. can crushed
pineapple, drained
2 cups (8 ozs.) shredded
cheddar cheese

½ cup chopped pecans
¼ cup chopped dried
apricots
1 teaspoon chopped
crystallized ginger

Combine softened cream cheese and pineapple, mixing until well blended. Add remaining ingredients; mix well. Chill. Shape into log. Serve with sesame crackers.

Variation: Just before serving, roll the log in chopped nuts or toasted sesame seeds.

Party Cheese Ball

A Kraft "classic" and everybody's favorite cheese ball—a savory attraction for any gathering, casual to formal.

2 8-oz. pkgs. Philadelphia Brand cream cheese

2 cups (8 ozs.) shredded Cracker Barrel sharp cheddar cheese

1 tablespoon chopped pimiento

1 tablespoon chopped green pepper

1 tablespoon finely chopped onion

2 teaspoons Worcestershire sauce

1 teaspoon lemon juice

Dash of cayenne

Dash of salt

Finely chopped pecans

Combine softened cream cheese and cheddar cheese, mixing until well blended. Add pimiento, green pepper, onion, Worcestershire sauce, lemon juice and seasonings; mix well. Chill. Shape into ball; roll in nuts. Serve with crackers.

During the party season, leftover cheese ball can be re-shaped and refrigerated until the next event.

Liptauer Spread

An Austrian original, this cream cheese mixture is zesty with the flavors of onion, anchovy, mustard, and caraway.

1 8-oz. pkg. cream cheese

½ cup soft Parkay margarine

2 tablespoons finely chopped onion

1½ teaspoons anchovy paste

1 teaspoon prepared mustard

1 teaspoon capers, chopped

1 teaspoon caraway seed

1 teaspoon paprika

Combine softened cream cheese and margarine, mixing until well blended. Add remaining ingredients; mix well. Chill. Serve with French or pumpernickel bread. 1½ cups

Variation: For a make-your-own appetizer arrangement, omit onion, anchovy paste and capers. Surround the spread with bowls of chopped onion, chives, anchovies and capers. Serve with assorted breads and crackers; let your guests make their own appetizers.

Burning Bush

This Kraft "classic" dates back to the 1930s. Today as then, dried beef and cream cheese are a popular combination.

1 8-oz. pkg. Philadelphia Brand cream cheese Dried beef, finely chopped	Grapefruit or large apple

Divide cream cheese into 24 pieces. Shape into balls; roll in dried beef. Place balls on picks; insert in grapefruit. 24 balls

Variation: Substitute finely chopped nuts for the dried beef.

Crispy Cheese Wafers

A modern version of a Kraft Kitchens original, Cheese Straws. Serve these crispy wafers as an appetizer, or as an accompaniment to main dish salads, soups or chowders.

2 cups (8 ozs.) shredded Kraft sharp cheddar cheese	1 teaspoon Worcestershire sauce
1/3 cup margarine	1/4 teaspoon salt
	1 cup flour

Thoroughly blend cheese and margarine; stir in Worcestershire sauce and salt. Add flour; mix well. Shape into two rolls, 1½ inches in diameter. Wrap securely; chill several hours or overnight. Cut rolls into ¼-inch slices; place on lightly greased cookie sheet. Bake at 375°, 10 to 12 minutes. 4 dozen

Curried Pecans

These spicy nibblers are an easy do-ahead for any festive occasion.

1/4 cup Squeeze Parkay margarine	1 teaspoon salt
1 teaspoon curry powder	4 cups (1 lb.) pecan halves

Combine margarine and seasonings. Add nuts; mix well. Spread on ungreased 15½ × 10½-inch jelly roll pan. Bake at 350°, 10 to 12 minutes, stirring occasionally.

To serve warm, pop in a 350° oven for a few minutes just before serving.

Manhattan Meatballs

A hearty, hot sweet-sour appetizer for a crowd—another time, serve as an entrée with fluffy rice and a tossed green salad.

2 lbs. ground beef
2 cups soft bread crumbs
½ cup chopped onion
2 eggs
2 tablespoons chopped parsley

2 teaspoons salt
2 tablespoons margarine
1 10-oz. jar Kraft apricot preserves
½ cup barbecue sauce

Combine meat, crumbs, onion, eggs, parsley and salt; mix lightly. Shape into 1-inch meatballs. Brown in margarine; drain. Place in 2-quart casserole. Combine preserves and barbecue sauce; pour over meatballs. Bake at 350°, 30 minutes, stirring occasionally. Approximately 4½ dozen

To Make Ahead: Prepare recipe as directed, except for baking. Cover; seal securely. Freeze. When ready to serve, place in refrigerator 6 to 8 hours. Uncover; bake at 350°, 1 hour, stirring occasionally.

Quiche Lorraine

A French favorite, this cheese custard pie is traditionally baked in a fluted pan. It can also be served as a luncheon or supper main dish.

1 8-oz. pkg. Kraft Swiss cheese slices, cut into thin strips
2 tablespoons flour
1½ cups half and half
4 eggs, slightly beaten

8 crisply cooked bacon slices, crumbled
½ teaspoon salt
Dash of pepper
1 9-inch unbaked pastry shell

Toss cheese with flour. Add half and half, eggs, bacon and seasonings; mix well. Pour into pastry shell. Bake at 350°, 40 to 45 minutes or until set. 8 to 10 servings

Variation: Substitute ¾ cup chopped ham for bacon.

J. L. Kraft's frequently stated motto, "What we say we do, we do do!", was the underlying philosophy basic to all company operations.

Antipasto Genovese

Cheese, spicy meats and marinated vegetables are basic to any antipasto, a combination that automatically guarantees an attractive, colorful arrangement to tempt hungry diners.

Asparagus spears, cooked	Mushroom caps
Cauliflowerets, partially cooked	Kraft Italian dressing
Thin cucumber slices	Provolone cheese, sliced, cut into triangles
Pitted ripe olives	Salami slices
Cherry tomato halves	Lettuce

Place vegetables in separate containers; pour dressing over vegetables. Cover; marinate in refrigerator several hours or overnight. Drain. Arrange vegetables, cheese and salami on lettuce-covered platter.

In Italian, antipasto literally means "before the pasta," which coincides with the American appetizer course.

French Fried Camembert

Spectacular for a buffet appetizer party—the crispy brown crust and the melting cheese center are a delicious contrast.

1 5¼-oz. can Tiny Dane Danish camembert cheese	¼ cup dry bread crumbs
	1 egg, beaten
	Oil

Cut cheese into six wedges; coat with crumbs. Dip in egg; coat again with crumbs. Fry in deep hot oil, 350°, 3 to 5 minutes or until golden brown. Serve warm. 6 appetizers

Keep piping hot in a chafing dish or on a warming tray.

The method of producing process cheese consists of selecting and blending one or more natural cheeses followed by pasteurization and packaging. Pasteurization stops the aging process and improves the keeping quality.

Hot Crabmeat Puffs

A Kraft "classic" for the party of the year—save these for your most elegant entertaining. Preparation is somewhat time-consuming, so make ahead—they're definitely worth the effort.

1 8-oz. pkg. Philadelphia Brand cream cheese
1 tablespoon milk
½ teaspoon cream style horseradish
¼ teaspoon salt
Dash of pepper

1½ cups (7½-oz. can) flaked drained crabmeat
⅓ cup slivered almonds, toasted
2 tablespoons finely chopped onion
Miniature Cream Puffs

Combine softened cream cheese, milk, horseradish, salt and pepper, mixing until well blended. Add crabmeat, nuts and onion; mix well. Cut tops from Miniature Cream Puffs; fill puffs with crabmeat mixture. Replace tops. Bake at 375°, 10 minutes.

Miniature Cream Puffs

½ cup water
¼ cup margarine
½ cup flour

Dash of salt
2 eggs

Bring water and margarine to a boil. Add flour and salt; stir vigorously over low heat until mixture forms a ball. Remove from heat. Add eggs, one at a time, beating well after each addition. Drop rounded teaspoonfuls of batter onto ungreased cookie sheet. Bake at 400°, 30 to 35 minutes. Remove immediately from cookie sheet. 36 appetizers

To Make Ahead: Prepare recipe as directed. Wrap securely; freeze. Unwrap; bake at 375°, 30 minutes.

Until the advent of packaged cheese products, the cheese department in most grocery stores was simple and unprofitable. Traditionally, a large wheel of cheese stood on the counter under a glass bell. When a customer purchased cheese, a slice was cut from the huge round. Unfortunately, the cut surfaces dried out over night and were cut off and discarded the next morning — along with potential profits.

Quick and Easy Appetizers

Put these together in no time at all—serve with pride and pleasure.

- Marinate shrimp in Kraft Italian dressing for several hours in the refrigerator. Drain and arrange on picks with pitted ripe olives.

- Spread thin ham slices with Philadelphia Brand Whipped cream cheese. Roll up and chill. Cut into 1½-inch pieces.

- Marinate fresh mushroom caps and artichoke hearts in Kraft caesar dressing for several hours in the refrigerator. Drain and serve on picks.

- Spread thin slices of French bread with soft margarine. Top with Kraft shredded mozzarella cheese. Heat at 350° until cheese melts.

- Combine flaked crabmeat with enough Kraft real mayonnaise to moisten. Season lightly with curry powder. Serve as a spread with melba toast or sesame crackers.

- Serve melon balls, pineapple chunks and apple wedges as dippers with Kraft blue cheese sour cream dip.

- Spread an 8-oz. pkg. Philadelphia Brand cream cheese with chutney and serve with crackers.

- Stuff large mushroom caps with Philadelphia Brand Whipped cream cheese—with bacon and horseradish, chives or onions.

- Simmer cocktail sausages, ham or luncheon meat cubes in Kraft barbecue sauce. Keep warm in chafing dish or over a warmer.

- Sauté shrimp or scallops in Squeeze Parkay margarine. Season with dill weed. Serve in chafing dish or over a warmer.

- Spread melba toast with margarine and sprinkle with Kraft grated parmesan cheese. Toast in a 400° oven until golden brown.

The Kraft Story

1916–1927

Kraft's rapid growth and expansion were evident during these years. Operations were extended to the Pacific Coast areas. The first national cheese advertising appeared and Kraft became a household word in homes where cheese had never been used.

In 1921, Kraft introduced the revolutionary five-pound loaf of pasteurized blended process cheese, packaged in a wooden box. This was a cheese product without rind or waste, bearing the identity and the guarantee of the maker—a cheese dependable in quality, uniform in flavor and texture, and with keeping qualities never before attained. It changed the nation's eating habits. Since that time, cheese consumption in the United States has risen from 4.16 pounds per person to 15.9 pounds in 1976.

The increased nationwide demand for cheese had a profound effect on the dairy industry. Cheese production areas had been concentrated in a few states, such as Wisconsin and New York. Increasing demand made it necessary to find new milk-producing areas to meet the growing needs of cheese production plants. J. L. Kraft successfully canvassed the country, encouraging farmers to produce more milk and assisting local agencies and dairymen in the development of efficient, workable programs. The result —milk and cheese production is now a major, nationwide industry. Kraft has expanded its own consulting program directed toward the development of sophisticated quality control and dairy methods.

By 1924, the company recognized the need for professional assistance to represent its prime concern—the consumer—and employed its first home economist. It was her responsibility to answer consumer inquiries about the company and its products and to keep management informed of consumer trends, needs, and expectations. Throughout the years, the responsibilities have expanded, paralleling the company's growth. Today, the Kraft Kitchens occupy a sixteen-room center located in the Chicago office and similar departments exist in Canada, England, Germany, Australia, and the Philippines. These departments have a wide range of responsibilities related to product development, labeling, recipe testing, food photography, advertising, sales promotion, education programs, and consumer information.

Snacks

Today's lifestyle — fast-paced, independent, and casual — has elevated snacks to a significant position in the daily diet. In fact surveys indicate that, for many, five or six planned snacks or mini-meals are replacing the traditional three-square-meals per day. Why? — because snacks are easy to prepare, can be eaten informally and quickly, and are more satisfying and less filling than hearty meals.

Whether snacks are a major part of the daily menu or simply a supplement to regular meals, they should be thoughtfully planned to provide nourishment and prevent weight gain from overeating. Almost all foods contain calories but not all provide the necessary nutrients — protein, carbohydrates, fats, vitamins, and minerals. The same basic food groups used in meal planning are good guides for preparing nourishing snacks. These groups — meat, dairy products, vegetable/fruit, and bread/cereal — offer a wide selection of foods for satisfying snacks.

With a little planning, snacks can be imaginative, appetizing, and nourishing. Whenever possible, partially or completely prepare snack foods in advance. This way, you are more inclined to consider nutritive value and appetite appeal. Many foods — such as sandwich spreads, dips, and salad mixtures actually improve if the flavors are allowed to blend overnight.

The range of ideas in this chapter includes pizza, cookies, dips, spreads, cheese and fruit, yogurt shakes, and sandwich fillings. Something for everyone!

Egg Salad Spread

A nourishing spread for active, growing children. Keep a supply on hand for a do-it-yourself snack on toast, crackers or celery sticks.

4 hard-cooked eggs,
   chopped
2 tablespoons sweet
   pickle relish, drained
1 tablespoon finely
   chopped onion

1 teaspoon prepared
   mustard
Miracle Whip salad
   dressing

Combine eggs, pickle relish, onion, mustard and enough salad dressing to moisten; mix lightly. 1⅓ cups

Variations: Add ½ cup (2 ozs.) shredded process American cheese or ¼ cup chopped celery. Substitute ¼ cup chopped stuffed green or pitted ripe olive slices for pickle relish.

The first five-pound loaf of pasteurized process American cheese was quickly followed to market by similar size loaves of pimento, Swiss, brick and Old English brand.

Devilish Good Eggs

An excellent snack for any age! Good do-ahead for parties, too—keep tightly covered in the refrigerator.

6 hard-cooked eggs
¼ cup Miracle Whip
   salad dressing

1 teaspoon prepared
   mustard
¼ teaspoon salt

Cut eggs in half. Remove yolks; mash. Blend in remaining ingredients; refill whites.

Variations: Add one of the following to egg yolk mixture—1 tablespoon pickle relish; or 3 crisply cooked bacon slices, crumbled; or 2 teaspoons chopped chives.

Refilling egg whites is easy and speedy if you use a pastry tube with a wide point.

Hearty Picnic Sticks

These good, satisfying snacks are really a sandwich in re-verse—make them with any type of luncheon meat.

Salami slices
Cheez Whiz process cheese
   spread

Bread sticks

For each snack, spread one salami slice with cheese spread; wrap around bread stick.

Festive Fall Fondue

Simple, delicious, ready in minutes—a treat that has great appetite appeal for teens. It makes a perfect snack for after-the-game gatherings or unexpected guests.

1 16-oz. jar Cheez Whiz
   process cheese
   spread

⅓ cup applesauce
¼ teaspoon cinnamon

Combine ingredients in fondue pot or saucepan; heat, stir-ring occasionally. Serve with French bread and apple chunks. 2 cups

Four O'Clock Munchers

A crock of this spread, stored in the refrigerator, provides a ready reserve for young athletes and other ardent snackers.

2 cups (8 ozs.) shredded
   Deluxe Choice
   process American
   cheese
¼ cup chopped green
   pepper

¼ cup chopped peanuts
½ cup salad dressing
   or mayonnaise
8 raisin or whole-wheat
   bread slices, toasted

Combine cheese, green pepper, nuts and salad dressing; mix lightly. For each sandwich, spread one slice of bread with cheese mixture. Broil until cheese is melted. 8 sandwiches

Variations: Varying the types of bread, nuts and cheese can provide almost infinite variety to suit any taste.

Mushroom Bread

A unique bread that resembles a pizza without sauce—serve as a snack anytime, or with a crisp tossed salad, scrambled eggs or a bowl of soup for a delightful lunch or late evening mini-meal.

1 8-oz. can refrigerated
   crescent rolls
2 cups mushroom slices
¼ cup margarine, melted

Kraft grated parmesan
   cheese
¼ teaspoon marjoram

Separate dough into triangles. Place on ungreased 12-inch pizza pan; press out dough to fit pan. Toss mushrooms with margarine; arrange on dough. Sprinkle with cheese and marjoram. Bake at 375°, 20 to 25 minutes.

Variations: Shredded mozzarella, monterey jack or Swiss cheese are excellent alternates for parmesan.

Cheddar Salami Stackups

Prepare these flavorful meat-cheese snacks in advance for easy entertaining—or for hungry young refrigerator raiders.

Salami slices
Cracker Barrel cheddar flavor cold pack cheese food

For each stackup, spread two slices of salami with cheese food. Stack slices; top with third slice. Chill. Cut into wedges; serve on picks.

Parmesan Sticks

For crisper sticks, bake a day in advance and store in a loosely covered container.

1 8-oz. can refrigerated
   crescent rolls

½ cup Kraft grated
   parmesan cheese

Separate dough into four rectangles; sprinkle both sides with cheese. On an unfloured surface, roll out each rectangle to a 7 × 4-inch rectangle. Cut into six lengthwise strips; cut each strip in half crosswise. Twist strips; place on greased cookie sheet. Bake at 375°, 6 to 8 minutes. 4 dozen

Fruit Dip Refresher

Keep a supply of this refreshing dip in the refrigerator and you won't have to lead hungry snackers to the fresh fruit.

½ cup mayonnaise
½ cup dairy sour cream

¼ cup Kraft orange
    marmalade or apricot
    preserves

Combine mayonnaise and sour cream; mix well. Stir in marmalade. Chill. Serve with fruit dippers such as banana and apple chunks, and orange and grapefruit segments. Approximately 1 cup

This dip can also be served as a dressing for fruit salads.

Parmesan Popcorn

Popcorn is everybody's favorite—bring out this cheese version, along with a jug of cider, as an instant snack for impromptu gatherings.

8 cups hot, freshly
    popped corn
¼ cup margarine, melted

Kraft grated parmesan
    cheese
Salt

Toss popcorn with margarine and cheese. Season to taste.

Save any leftovers for topping soups and tossed salads.

Mallow S'Mores

Indoor version of a favorite cookout treat.

Graham crackers
Peanut butter

Jets marshmallows

For each s'more, spread cracker with peanut butter. Top with marshmallow; broil until lightly browned. Press second cracker on top.

In 1924, the name of the company was changed to the Kraft Cheese Company and branch offices in Hamburg and Cologne, Germany, were opened. During the next two years, offices were opened in England and Australia.

Party Mix

A favorite that disappears in no time at any gathering.

⅔ cup Squeeze Parkay
  margarine
1 teaspoon
  Worcestershire sauce
½ teaspoon garlic salt
2 cups toasted oat cereal

2 cups bite-size crispy
  wheat squares
2 cups bite-size crispy
  rice squares
2 cups pretzel sticks
2 cups mixed nuts

Combine margarine, Worcestershire sauce and garlic salt. Pour over combined remaining ingredients; mix lightly. Spread on ungreased 15½ × 10½-inch jelly roll pan. Bake at 250°, 1 hour, stirring occasionally. Approximately 10 cups

Variation: Raisins and peanuts can be substituted for the oat cereal and mixed nuts.

Party mix can be prepared in advance and stored in a tightly covered container. Reheat briefly at 350°.

Quick Pizza Treats

These cheese-topped petite pizzas are popular snacks with the late-evening crowd—serve them hot (and often).

1 8-oz. can tomato sauce
2 tablespoons finely
  chopped green pepper
1 tablespoon finely
  chopped onion
¼ teaspoon oregano
  leaves, crushed

4 English muffins, split,
  toasted
4 Deluxe Choice process
  American cheese
  slices, cut in half

Combine tomato sauce, green pepper, onion and oregano. For each appetizer, spoon tomato mixture onto muffins; broil until hot. Top with cheese; continue broiling until melted. 8 servings

Variation: Substitute Swiss cheese slices, shredded mozzarella or grated parmesan cheese for American.

Bran Apple Cookies

Cookie jars never go out of style—keep yours filled with old-fashioned, nourishing treats like these.

1 cup flour
½ cup sugar
1 teaspoon cinnamon
¼ teaspoon soda
1 cup (4 ozs.) shredded
  Deluxe Choice•Old
  English process
  American cheese

2 cups bran flakes
1 cup chopped apple
½ cup Squeeze Parkay
  margarine
1 egg, beaten

Combine flour, sugar, cinnamon and soda. Add cheese, cereal and apple; mix lightly. Add margarine and egg, mixing just until moistened. Drop rounded tablespoonfuls of dough onto ungreased cookie sheet. Bake at 350°, 12 to 15 minutes. Approximately 2½ dozen

Sunshine Refresher

A nourishing eggnog to serve at breakfast or brunch, or as an afternoon snack.

1 cup Kraft marshmallow
  creme

3 cups orange juice
4 eggs

Blend marshmallow creme and ¼ cup orange juice in blender or at medium speed on electric mixer until smooth. Add remaining juice and eggs; beat until foamy. Eight ½-cup servings

Yogurt Fruit Shake

A nutritious snack or an instant breakfast for people on the go.

2 cups milk
1 8-oz. container plain
  yogurt
½ cup Kraft strawberry or
  apricot preserves

1 medium banana, cut
  into chunks

Place ingredients in blender container; blend on high speed until foamy. Serve cold. Eight ½-cup servings

Variation: Substitute ½ pint vanilla ice cream for yogurt.

Swiss Mix Sandwiches

A versatile sandwich filling to keep on hand for instant nourishing snacks—it's also delicious on sesame crackers, rye toast or celery sticks.

1½ cups (6 ozs.) shredded
    Kraft Swiss cheese
1½ cups shredded carrots
½ cup chopped nuts
⅓ cup raisins

Mayonnaise or salad
    dressing
12 whole-wheat or white
    bread slices

Combine cheese, carrots, nuts, raisins and enough mayonnaise to moisten; mix lightly. For each sandwich, spread two bread slices with mayonnaise; fill with cheese mixture. 6 sandwiches

To Make Ahead: Store filling in refrigerator, tightly covered.

Tomato Cheese Pizza

A great basic pizza with crisp golden crust, mildly seasoned sauce and the perfect Italian cheese—personalize with onion rings, mushroom slices, crumbled bacon, cooked sausage or ground beef, pepperoni.

2 cups flour
1 tablespoon baking
    powder
1 teaspoon salt
⅔ cup milk
⅓ cup oil

      *   *   *
1 6-oz. can tomato paste

¼ cup water
1 teaspoon oregano
    leaves, crushed
½ teaspoon salt
¼ teaspoon pepper
1 8-oz. pkg. Kraft
    mozzarella cheese
    slices, cut into strips

Combine dry ingredients; add milk and oil. Stir with fork until mixture forms a ball. On floured surface, knead dough about ten times. Roll out dough in 14-inch pizza pan.

Combine tomato paste, water and seasonings; spread on dough. Top with cheese. Bake at 425°, 15 to 20 minutes.

Instant Snacks

Made-in-a-jiffy morsels for family and friends.

- Spread whipped cream cheese on date-nut or Boston brown bread slices.

- Spear cubes of Velveeta process cheese spread with pretzel sticks.

- Stock a supply of crisp vegetables—carrot, cucumber, zucchini and celery sticks—and Kraft ready-to-serve dips—jalapeño pepper, blue cheese, dill pickle and onion.

- Spread toasted bagels with whipped cream cheese and top with shredded carrots, raisins, sliced cucumber, chopped nuts or olives.

- Marinate leftover cooked vegetables in Kraft low calorie Italian dressing or Catalina low calorie dressing and chill.

- Stuff celery with any flavor of whipped cream cheese—chive, blue cheese, bacon and horseradish.

- Top crackers, apple or pear wedges, or corn chips with Squeez-A-Snak process cheese spread—sharp, pimento or jalapeño pepper.

- Spread rye, raisin or whole-wheat toast with Cheez Whiz process cheese spread.

- Wrap a slice of cheese around a dill pickle or cucumber stick.

- Spread toasted English muffin halves with whipped cream cheese and orange marmalade.

- Wrap a lettuce leaf around a chunk of cheese.

- Stuff prunes or dates with cream cheese.

Once test kitchen facilities were installed, there was a change in Kraft magazine advertisements. Recipes, food ideas, and cooking tips were included. This has been the format for most Kraft ads since that time.

The Kraft Story

1928–1932

The late 1920s was a major transition period. In 1928, the Kraft Cheese Company merged with the Phenix Cheese Corporation and became the Kraft-Phenix Cheese Corporation. Then, in 1930, Kraft became an operating unit of the National Dairy Products Corporation. The benefits from these mergers were product diversification and expanded research, educational programs and advertising.

From 1928 to 1933, Kraft introduced several products that met with such immediate and lasting success that they are still some of our most popular products.

In 1928, a major product innovation was Velveeta pasteurized process cheese spread. It was a completely new type of cheese product made by blending mild natural cheese with milk solids and whey, a nutritious ingredient normally lost in the manufacture of natural cheese. The result was a highly nourishing product with a mild flavor and smooth texture—destined to become the most popular American-type cheese product in the United States.

Next came a product that would become the largest selling packaged cheese in the world—Philadelphia Brand cream cheese. It was first introduced at Chester, New York in 1872 and was later named Philadelphia Brand. In the late nineteenth century, Philadelphia was considered a home of fine food, thus it seemed an appropriate name for a premium quality cheese.

Beginning in 1928, Kraft French dressing and mayonnaise were the first of a long line of salad products to be introduced. The year 1932 marked the beginning of a spectacular success story. Miracle Whip salad dressing, a product that combined the best features of mayonnaise and old-fashioned boiled dressing, was test marketed. Within one year, Miracle Whip salad dressing was in national distribution and outselling the next twenty competitive brands combined. For the first time salads began to be served regularly in homes throughout the nation.

Soups, Stews, and Chowders

Soups and their near relatives, stews and chowders, have always held a prominent position in traditional American cuisine. In the earliest pioneer days, succulent meats and vegetables continually simmered in a large iron kettle over an open hearth, always ready to provide nourishment for the hard-working family. The regional specialties that evolved were dependent on native bounty and produce — turkey, duck, venison, bear, possum, corn, squash, potatoes, rice, okra, herbs, and spices.

Today, soups are still one of our most versatile foods and are considered appropriate fare for almost any occasion, meal, or season. Small portions of light creamy soups or broths are served as an appetizer or first course. Hearty soups or chowders are appropriate for lunch or supper — in fact soup and a sandwich for lunch is an American tradition. Chili, thick meat or fish stew, or robust vegetable chowders are especially welcomed on cold wintry days. An added bonus — soups are great do-aheads for parties or busy days.

Hot or cold — light or hearty — clear or creamy, soups are an easy way of serving nutritious foods in an imaginative manner. Meats, vegetables, pasta, cheese, almost any food is suitable for soup. Leftover foods, especially, take on new appeal when combined in a flavorful chowder or stew.

For inspiration, try any of the Kraft originals on the following pages.

Cheemato Soup

This was the first recipe to introduce the nation to Cheez Whiz process cheese spread in 1953. Both the recipe and the product have been favorites ever since.

1 10¾-oz. can condensed tomato soup
1¼ cups water

1 8-oz. jar Cheez Whiz process cheese spread
Dash of pepper

Combine soup and water; heat. Add remaining ingredients; stir until smooth. Four ¾-cup servings

Variations: Add one 6½-oz. can tuna, or 2 tablespoons sherry.

Cheese 'n Ale Soup

An import from the English Kraft Kitchens—cheddar cheese and ale (or beer) make this hearty soup distinctively British.

⅔ cup shredded carrots
¼ cup chopped onion
¼ cup margarine
¼ cup flour
   Dash of salt and pepper

2½ cups milk
2 cups (8 ozs.) shredded Kraft sharp cheddar cheese
½ cup ale or beer

Sauté vegetables in margarine. Blend in flour and seasonings. Gradually add milk; cook, stirring constantly, until thickened. Add cheese; stir until melted. Add ale. Heat; do not boil. Four 1-cup servings

Variation: Substitute 8 ounces Velveeta process cheese spread, cubed, or process American cheese, shredded, for cheddar cheese.

In the 1920s, Kraft was concerned about the loss of nutrients when whey and milk solids were drained from the vat during cheesemaking, and vanished down the drain. Research experts tried adding the milk solids back into the cheese and the resulting product was Velveeta pasteurized process cheese spread. It was softer than natural or process cheese — delicious and nutritious.

Gazpacho

This appealing appetizer soup, served cold, departs from the traditional Spanish version by replacing olive oil and seasoning with French dressing.

4 cups tomato juice
½ cup Catalina French
  dressing
½ cup finely chopped
  onion
½ cup finely chopped
  green pepper
½ cup finely chopped
  peeled tomato
½ cup finely chopped
  peeled cucumber

Combine ingredients; chill. Serve in glasses or bouillon cups. Twelve ½-cup servings

Gazpacho aficionados—and there are many—keep a chilled supply on hand during the hot summer months for instant refreshment. For guests, the soup can be attractively presented in a large bowl or pitcher, surrounded by small bowls of croutons, chopped onion, green pepper and tomato.

Parisian Onion Soup

Quick, easy, and very French, this hearty and handsome onion soup can be served as a substantial first course or as the main dish at lunch. Don't be stingy with the cheese!

3 cups onion rings
2 tablespoons margarine
4 cups beef broth
  Dash of pepper
4 French bread slices,
  toasted
Kraft Swiss cheese,
  shredded
Kraft grated parmesan
  cheese

Sauté onion in margarine. Add broth and pepper. Cover; simmer 15 minutes. Pour soup into bowls; top with toast. Cover with Swiss and parmesan cheese; broil until melted. Serve immediately. Four 1-cup servings

Variation: Substitute shredded mozzarella cheese for Swiss.

Toast and cheese should be added just before serving so that the toast remains crisp and the cheese is freshly melted. Add as much cheese as you wish—the French like it bubbling over the top of the bowl.

Creme Vichyssoise

An elegant appetizer soup traditionally served in small bowls nestled in a bed of crushed ice. The special feature that makes this a Kraft "classic" is cream cheese.

4 cups chicken broth or
    bouillon
4 cups chopped potatoes
¼ cup onion slices
1½ teaspoons salt

1 8-oz. pkg. Philadelphia
    Brand cream cheese
1 tablespoon finely
    chopped chives

In large saucepan, combine broth, potatoes, onion and salt. Cover; simmer 20 minutes or until potatoes are very tender. Force mixture through sieve. Gradually add mixture to softened cream cheese, mixing until well blended. Stir in chives; chill. Garnish with additional chives. Twelve ½-cup servings

This Creme Vichyssoise is equally appealing served warm.

Tomato Clam Bisque

This intriguing bisque is as simple as 1, 2, 3—open two cans (tomato soup, clams) and a jar (Cheez Whiz), combine and heat to serve as an appetizer course or a luncheon main dish.

1 10¾-oz. can condensed
    tomato soup
⅔ cup water
1 8-oz. jar Cheez Whiz
    process cheese spread

1 8-oz. can minced clams,
    drained
1 to 2 tablespoons sherry

Combine soup and water; heat. Add remaining ingredients; stir until smooth. Four ¾-cup servings

Serve Tomato Clam Bisque with Dainty Herb Crescents and Spinach Salad.

During the twenties, the sales force had built a distribution system to service perishable cheese products. Kraft made additional use of its trucks when it introduced a line of salad dressings, another highly perishable product. This was the beginning of a long line of fine dressings.

Zucchini Bisque

This delicate, creamy soup is equally appealing hot or cold —an excellent summer recipe, using garden-fresh zucchini.

2 cups chopped zucchini	1 chicken bouillon cube
1 cup water	⅛ teaspoon basil
½ cup tomato juice	1 8-oz. pkg. Philadelphia
1 tablespoon chopped	Brand cream cheese,
onion	cubed

In saucepan, combine ingredients except cream cheese. Cover; simmer 20 minutes. Pour into blender. Add cream cheese; blend until smooth. Return to saucepan; heat thoroughly. Six ½-cup servings

Harvest Stew

Beef, vegetables and a zesty sauce topped with easy-do dumplings — a one dish meal for family or guests.

2 lbs. round steak, ¾ inch thick	3 medium onions, quartered
2 tablespoons oil	1 teaspoon salt
2½ cups water	¼ cup flour
1 cup Kraft barbecue sauce	3 medium zucchini, cut into ½-inch slices
8 carrots, halved	1 cup all purpose biscuit mix

Cut meat into thin strips. In large Dutch oven, brown meat in oil. Add 2 cups water, barbecue sauce, carrots, onions and salt. Cover; simmer 1 hour. Gradually add remaining water to flour, stirring until well blended. Gradually add flour mixture to hot meat and vegetables, stirring constantly until mixture boils and thickens. Add zucchini. Prepare biscuit mix as directed on package for dumplings. Drop rounded tablespoonfuls onto hot stew mixture. Simmer 10 minutes. Cover; continue simmering 15 minutes. 6 to 8 servings

To Make Ahead: Prepare stew in advance except for zucchini and dumplings; reheat, adding zucchini and dumplings during the last 25 minutes.

Sorrento Stew

This modern "minestrone" is extra easy, because it's made with Italian spaghetti dinner—the pasta, traditional season- ings and parmesan cheese come complete in one package.

1 lb. mild Italian sausage
1 pkg. Kraft Italian
   spaghetti dinner
1 29-oz. can tomatoes
1 16-oz. can kidney
   beans, drained

1 cup chopped green
   pepper
½ cup chopped onion
1 6-oz. can tomato paste
3 cups water

Remove casing from sausage. In Dutch oven, brown sausage; drain. Add the herb-spice mix, vegetables, tomato paste and water; bring to boil. Break the spaghetti into thirds; add to hot mixture. Cover; simmer 20 minutes. Sprinkle servings with the grated parmesan cheese. 6 to 8 servings

Western Stew

Marinating the beef in a spicy tomato dressing turns a basic stew into something very special.

1 8-oz. bottle Catalina
   French dressing
2 lbs. beef, cut into
   1-inch cubes
2¼ cups water

4 small potatoes,
   quartered
1½ cups carrot slices
2 small onions, quartered
¼ cup flour

Pour dressing over meat. Cover; marinate in refrigerator several hours or overnight. Drain, reserving marinade. In Dutch oven, brown meat over low heat. Add marinade and 2 cups water. Cover; simmer 2 hours. Add vegetables; con- tinue simmering 45 minutes or until vegetables are tender. Gradually add remaining water to flour, stirring until well blended. Gradually add flour mixture to hot meat and vege- tables, stirring constantly until mixture boils and thickens. Simmer 3 minutes, stirring constantly. 6 to 8 servings

For accompaniment, serve Cheese Bread, a crisp green salad, and Mocha Tortoni.

Chili con Queso

By now a national institution, chili originated in the south-west when cowboys dined on chuckwagon fare cooked in over-the-fire kettles. Its popularity has never wavered—and the variations are almost unlimited.

1 lb. ground beef
½ cup chopped onion
1 16-oz. can kidney beans, undrained
1 16-oz. can tomatoes, undrained

1 8-oz. can tomato sauce
1 tablespoon chili powder
1 teaspoon salt
Kraft sharp cheddar cheese, shredded

Brown meat; drain. Add onion; cook until tender. Stir in remaining ingredients except cheese. Cover; simmer 30 minutes, stirring occasionally. Top with cheese. 4 servings

Variation: Cook ½ cup chopped green pepper with the onion and add ¼ cup dry red wine.

Corn Chili

Midwestern version of an American tradition—corn is the unique ingredient.

1 lb. ground beef
½ cup chopped onion
1 tablespoon chili powder
1 teaspoon salt
1 28-oz. can tomatoes, undrained

1 16-oz. can kidney beans, undrained
1 12-oz. can corn, undrained
1 cup Kraft barbecue sauce

In Dutch oven, brown meat; drain. Add onion and seasonings; cook until onion is tender. Stir in remaining ingredients. Cover; simmer 20 minutes. 8 servings

Serve with an assorted fruit and cheese tray and heated Kaiser rolls.

During this period of expansion, 1928–1932, Kraft product introductions included thousand island dressing, Old English and olive cheese spreads in jars, and grated American cheese — still existing products a half century later.

Pueblo Chili

Authentic New Mexican chili made with lamb and garbanzo beans indigenous to the area. Barbecue sauce provides the seasoning.

2 lbs. lamb or beef, cut
    into 1-inch cubes
Oil
2 cups chopped onion
2 cups water
½ cup Kraft regular or
    hot barbecue sauce

1 teaspoon salt
2 16-oz. cans garbanzo
    beans, undrained
4 green peppers, cut into
    2-inch squares

Brown meat in oil; drain. Add onion, water, barbecue sauce and salt. Cover; simmer 1 hour. Stir in beans and green pepper; cook 15 minutes or until meat is tender. 6 servings

Serve with cornbread and a fresh fruit salad.

Midwest Chowder

A Kraft "classic" that has been a perennial favorite since the late 1950s.

2 cups boiling water
2 cups chopped potatoes
½ cup carrot slices
½ cup celery slices
¼ cup chopped onion
1½ teaspoons salt
¼ teaspoon pepper
¼ cup margarine

¼ cup flour
2 cups milk
2½ cups (10 ozs.) shredded
    Cracker Barrel sharp
    cheddar cheese
1 17-oz. can cream style
    corn

In large Dutch oven, combine water, vegetables and seasonings. Cover; simmer 10 minutes. Do not drain. Make a white sauce with margarine, flour and milk. Add cheese; stir until melted. Add corn and undrained vegetables. Heat; do not boil. 6 to 8 servings

For variety, add one cup ham cubes, chopped cooked chicken or turkey, or flaked cooked cod or haddock.

44

Shrimp Cheese Chowder

Seafood-cheddar chowder for entertaining the après-ski or skating bunch—just right for a cold winter evening.

2 cups thin onion slices
2 tablespoons margarine
2 tablespoons flour
1½ teaspoons salt
¼ teaspoon pepper
1½ cups water
2 cups chopped potatoes
1 cup celery slices

3 cups (1 lb.) cleaned, cooked shrimp
2 cups milk
2 cups (8 ozs.) shredded Kraft sharp cheddar cheese
2 tablespoons sherry

Sauté onion in margarine. Blend in flour and seasonings. Gradually add water; stir in vegetables. Cover; simmer 20 minutes. Add remaining ingredients; stir until cheese is melted. 6 to 8 servings

This chowder can be prepared in advance, then warmed gently over low to medium heat. Serve with warm French bread and a spinach salad.

School Day Chowder

A hearty lunch for the brown-bagging crowd, this will stay warm for hours in a tightly covered vacuum container.

½ lb. frankfurters, sliced
1 cup celery slices
½ cup carrot slices
½ cup chopped green pepper
¼ cup chopped onion
¼ cup margarine

¼ cup flour
Dash of pepper
2½ cups milk
2 cups (8 ozs.) shredded Kraft sharp cheddar cheese

Sauté frankfurters and vegetables in margarine. Blend in flour and pepper. Gradually add milk; cook, stirring constantly, until thickened. Add cheese and stir until melted. 6 servings

Pack fresh fruit and a few cookies to make a complete meal.

The Kraft Story

1933–1940

The year 1933 ushered in Kraft's golden era of radio. The first "Kraft Music Hall," a musical and variety radio program, was conducted by Paul Whiteman, and had Al Jolson as a guest entertainer. This popular program continued through 1949 and featured such notables as Bing Crosby, Eddie Duchin, John Scott Trotter, Nelson Eddy, Shirley Temple, Bob Burns, The Mills Brothers, and Mary Martin.

The thirties were also a remarkable era for product expansion. Swankyswigs (process cheese spread in decorative glasses), Parkay margarine, Kraft macaroni and cheese dinner, and caramels were introduced in rapid succession.

Swankyswigs represented the first attempt to market cheese spreads in attractive reusable glasses. They are still a promotional success and the original glasses are now collectors' items. The colorful designs have been changed several times in response to consumer requests for new patterns.

Parkay margarine was introduced in 1937, but was not in national distribution until 1940. Margarine was known originally as oleomargarine and was white in color. Packages of Parkay margarine contained packets of coloring which could be added by the consumer. Commercially colored margarine was not available until 1948, when several states revised their food laws to permit the addition of color by the manufacturer.

Kraft's first attempt to market a macaroni and cheese product was in 1922. However, it was not until 1936 when a quick-cooking macaroni was developed, that Kraft macaroni and cheese dinner was launched into national distribution. This product initiated the trend of complete-meal-in-a-package foods which is characteristic of today's lifestyle. Its versatility, economy, convenience, and quick preparation are other qualities that still have special appeal after 40 years.

Kraft caramels by the bag were first introduced in 1938. Although they were marketed as a confection, it wasn't long before Kraft home economists developed new uses for the product. Caramel Apples, Caramel Popcorn Balls, Caramel Pecan Pie, and Caramel Sauce were soon popular recipes.

The 1930s set the pace for the development of diversified food products to meet consumer expectations. This is still a guiding philosophy for Kraft research and marketing operations.

Breads and Coffee Cakes

Along with other old-fashioned skills, bread baking is enjoying a tremendous revival. People everywhere are experiencing the deep satisfaction that comes from kneading the dough, shaping the loaves, and anticipating the results — and their families are reaping the benefits of freshly-made bread in its many forms and varieties.

America's diverse cultural heritage has produced an almost limitless selection of muffins, biscuits, rolls, yeast and quick breads. In this chapter, you'll find such specialties as Irish Soda Bread, Sally Lunn, Panettone, Lemon Tree Muffins, and Cheddar Quick Bread. Some are quick and easy, made from refrigerated doughs. Others are designed for a day of leisurely baking.

A few quick and easy tips will help insure success. Check the date on yeast packages. (Dry yeast will keep several months in a cool dry place.) Cover rising dough with a damp cloth, waxed paper, or an inverted bowl. The dough is proofed when it is double in bulk and dome shaped with small bubbles just below the surface. Unless directions indicate thorough mixing, combine ingredients for quick-type breads just until the dry ingredients are completely moistened. For a soft tender crust, brush bread or rolls with melted margarine just after removing from the oven.

Whether you bake alone, with a friend, or involve the family in a complete event, you will find that bread baking is its own reward.

Apple Kuchen

An adaptation of a recipe from the Kraft Kitchens in Germany—serve this rich coffee cake at breakfast, brunch or teatime.

½ cup Parkay margarine
1¾ cups sugar
2 eggs
1 teaspoon vanilla
3 cups flour
2 teaspoons baking powder

1 teaspoon salt
1 cup milk
3 cups peeled apple slices
1 teaspoon cinnamon

Cream margarine and 1½ cups sugar until light and fluffy. Blend in eggs and vanilla. Add combined dry ingredients to creamed mixture alternately with milk, mixing well after each addition. Pour into greased 13 × 9-inch baking pan. Arrange apples on top. Sprinkle with combined remaining sugar and cinnamon. Bake at 375°, 35 to 40 minutes.

Apricot Crumble Cake

Cream cheese is the special feature that adds a unique flavor and freshness to this elegant coffee cake.

1¼ cups granulated sugar
1 8-oz. pkg. cream cheese
½ cup margarine
2 eggs
1 teaspoon vanilla
2 cups sifted cake flour
1 teaspoon baking powder
½ teaspoon soda
¼ teaspoon salt

¼ cup milk
1 10-oz. jar Kraft apricot or peach preserves

* * *

2 cups shredded coconut
⅔ cup packed brown sugar
⅓ cup margarine, melted
1 teaspoon cinnamon

Combine granulated sugar, softened cream cheese and margarine, mixing until well blended. Blend in eggs and vanilla. Sift together dry ingredients. Add to cream cheese mixture alternately with milk, mixing well after each addition. Pour half of batter into greased and floured 13 × 9-inch baking pan. Dot with preserves; cover with remaining batter. Bake at 350°, 35 to 40 minutes.

Combine coconut, brown sugar, margarine and cinnamon; mix well. Spread on cake; broil until golden brown.

48

Coffee-Time Cake

A popular Kraft television recipe, this is a particular favorite with children—but no one can resist the terrific combination of bananas, cream cheese and pecans.

1¼ cups sugar
  1 8-oz. pkg. Philadelphia Brand cream cheese
  ½ cup margarine
  2 eggs
  1 cup mashed ripe bananas
  1 teaspoon vanilla

2¼ cups flour
1½ teaspoons baking powder
½ teaspoon soda

* * *

1 cup chopped pecans
2 tablespoons sugar
1 teaspoon cinnamon

Combine sugar, softened cream cheese and margarine, mixing until well blended. Add eggs, one at a time, mixing well after each addition. Blend in bananas and vanilla. Add combined flour, baking powder and soda; mix well. Combine nuts, sugar and cinnamon; fold half of mixture into batter. Pour into greased and floured 13 × 9-inch baking pan; top with remaining nut mixture. Bake at 350°, 35 to 40 minutes.

Crumb Top Coffee Cake

A Kraft "classic" that dates back to the late 1940s.

1½ cups flour
  1 cup packed brown sugar
  ½ cup Parkay margarine
1½ teaspoons baking powder

½ teaspoon cinnamon
½ teaspoon salt
⅔ cup milk
  1 egg, beaten

Combine flour and sugar; cut in ¼ cup margarine until mixture resembles coarse crumbs. Reserve 1 cup for topping. Add baking powder, cinnamon and salt; cut in remaining margarine. Add combined milk and egg, mixing just until moistened. Pour into greased and floured 8-inch square pan; sprinkle with reserved crumbs. Bake at 375°, 35 to 40 minutes. Serve warm.

This became a favorite with many families when Kraft sponsored its first television program, Kraft Theater, and initiated the famous how-to-do commercials.

Caramel Breakfast Cake

A Kraft television favorite of the early 1950s, with a convenience update. Caramel topping now replaces the melted caramels of the earlier version.

2 tablespoons sugar	2 8-oz. pkgs. refrigerated
¼ cup chopped pecans	biscuits
¾ cup Kraft caramel	⅓ cup margarine, melted
topping	

Sprinkle sugar on bottom of well-greased 9-inch layer pan; cover with nuts. Pour topping over nuts. Dip biscuits in margarine; arrange in pan with fifteen biscuits overlapping around outer edge and five in center. Bake at 400°, 23 to 25 minutes. Let stand 5 minutes; invert onto serving plate. Serve warm.

"Philly" Brunch Cake

This Kraft "classic" first appeared in our television commercials during the early 1950s and has continued to be a popular favorite.

⅓ cup packed brown	½ cup margarine
sugar	2 eggs
⅓ cup flour	1 teaspoon vanilla
½ teaspoon cinnamon	1¾ cups flour
2 tablespoons margarine	1 teaspoon baking
* * *	powder
1¼ cups granulated sugar	½ teaspoon soda
1 8-oz. pkg. Philadelphia	¼ teaspoon salt
Brand cream cheese	¼ cup milk

Combine dry ingredients; cut in margarine until mixture resembles coarse crumbs.

Combine granulated sugar, softened cream cheese and margarine, mixing until well blended. Blend in eggs and vanilla. Add combined dry ingredients to cream cheese mixture alternately with milk, mixing well after each addition. Pour into greased and floured 13 × 9-inch baking pan. Sprinkle with crumb mixture. Bake at 350°, 35 to 40 minutes.

Consumers quickly discovered that coffee cakes made with cream cheese are especially light, moist and flavorful.

Crunchy Brunch Biscuits

Quick, easy, and absolutely delicious, these spicy biscuits bake together for a pull-apart coffee cake effect, or separately as crispy rolls.

1 10-oz. can refrigerated biscuits
¼ cup Parkay margarine, melted

⅓ cup sugar
¼ teaspoon cinnamon

Dip biscuits in margarine; coat with combined sugar and cinnamon. Arrange in greased 9-inch layer pan. Bake at 375°, 20 to 25 minutes. Remove from pan immediately; serve warm. 10 biscuits

Variations: Add ⅓ cup chopped nuts and 1 tablespoon orange or lemon rind to sugar mixture.

For individual rolls, place prepared biscuits on ungreased cookie sheet. Bake at 375°, 12 minutes.

Blueberry Muffins

Who doesn't like warm, fragrant blueberry muffins?

2 cups flour
⅓ cup sugar
2 teaspoons baking powder
½ teaspoon salt
¾ cup milk

½ cup Parkay margarine, melted
1 egg
½ cup fresh or well-drained frozen blueberries

Combine dry ingredients. Add combined milk, margarine and egg, mixing just until moistened. Fold in blueberries. Pour into greased medium-size muffin pan, filling each cup ⅔ full. Bake at 425°, 20 to 25 minutes. 12 muffins

When you're in a baking mood, make several batches and freeze some for the future—rewarm at 350° or in a microwave oven.

In 1936, Bing Crosby became the star of the "Kraft Music Hall" and remained the host until 1946.

Cranberry Nut Bread

Served hot or cold, it's delicious. Makes a colorful holiday gift for your friends—add a container of whipped cream cheese for an extra treat.

⅓ cup **Parkay margarine**
1¼ cups **sugar**
2 **eggs**
3 cups **flour**
1 tablespoon **baking powder**
1 teaspoon **salt**
½ teaspoon **soda**

¾ cup **water**
⅓ cup **orange juice**
1½ cups **cranberries, coarsely chopped**
½ cup **chopped nuts**
1 tablespoon **grated orange rind**

Cream margarine and sugar until light and fluffy. Add eggs, one at a time, mixing well after each addition. Add combined dry ingredients alternately with water and orange juice, mixing well after each addition. Fold in cranberries, nuts and orange rind. Pour into greased and floured 9 × 5-inch loaf pan. Bake at 350°, 1 hour and 15 minutes. Cool 5 minutes; remove from pan.

Irish Soda Bread

A traditional Irish specialty also known as "Freckle Bread." Serve warm with marmalade and whipped cream cheese.

3¼ cups **flour**
¼ cup **sugar**
1 teaspoon **baking powder**
1 teaspoon **soda**

¾ teaspoon **salt**
½ cup **Parkay margarine**
1⅓ cups **buttermilk**
⅓ cup **currants or raisins**

Combine dry ingredients; cut in margarine until mixture resembles coarse crumbs. Add buttermilk and currants, mixing just until moistened. Shape into ball. On floured surface, knead dough ten times. Shape into round loaf; place on greased cookie sheet. Cut deep cross in top. Bake at 350°, 1 hour. Serve warm.

Variation: Roll round loaf in sugar before placing on cookie sheet.

Lemon Tree Muffins

Crunchy topping and fragrant citrus aroma make these festive and delectable. Versatile enough for any meal, a perfect companion for fruit salads.

½ cup Parkay margarine
½ cup sugar
1 teaspoon grated lemon rind
2 eggs, separated
1 cup flour
1 teaspoon baking powder

¼ teaspoon salt
3 tablespoons lemon juice

* * *

¼ cup chopped nuts
1 tablespoon sugar
1 teaspoon nutmeg

Cream margarine and sugar until light and fluffy. Blend in lemon rind. Add egg yolks, one at a time, mixing well after each addition. Add combined dry ingredients to creamed mixture alternately with lemon juice, mixing just until moistened. Fold in stiffly beaten egg whites. Spoon into greased medium-size muffin pan, filling each cup ½ full.

Sprinkle with combined nuts, sugar and nutmeg. Bake at 375°, 20 to 25 minutes. 12 muffins

Orange Marmalade Nut Bread

This recipe, almost as old as the Kraft Kitchens, has been a steady favorite through the years—makes a welcome after-school treat for the junior set.

½ cup margarine
½ cup packed brown sugar
2 eggs
1 10-oz. jar Kraft orange marmalade
2¾ cups flour

2 teaspoons baking powder
1 teaspoon salt
½ teaspoon soda
½ cup Kraft orange juice
½ cup chopped nuts

Cream margarine and sugar until light and fluffy. Add eggs, one at a time, mixing well after each addition. Blend in marmalade. Add combined dry ingredients to creamed mixture alternately with orange juice, mixing well after each addition. Stir in nuts. Spoon into greased 9 × 5-inch loaf pan. Bake at 325°, 1 hour and 20 minutes. Cool 5 minutes; remove from pan.

54

Jazzberry Muffins

Delicate muffin with an easy fruit filling—preserves! Colorful and attractive for any occasion.

2¼ cups flour
⅓ cup sugar
1 tablespoon baking powder
¾ teaspoon salt

¾ cup milk
⅓ cup oil
2 eggs
⅓ cup Kraft strawberry preserves

Combine dry ingredients. Add combined milk, oil and eggs, mixing just until moistened. Pour into greased medium-size muffin pan, filling each cup ½ full. Dot generously with preserves; top with remaining batter. Bake at 400°, 20 to 25 minutes. 12 muffins

Cheese Biscuits

These crusty biscuits complement almost any meal, any time of the day.

2 cups all purpose biscuit mix

1½ cups (6 ozs.) shredded Kraft sharp cheddar cheese

Prepare biscuit mix as directed on package for rolled biscuits; stir in cheese. On lightly floured surface, knead dough ten times. Roll to ½-inch thickness; cut with floured 3-inch cutter. Place on ungreased cookie sheet. Bake at 450°, 10 to 12 minutes. 10 to 12 biscuits

Rye Lace

Crisp curls of party rye bread—deliciously crunchy.

Unsliced party rye bread   Parkay margarine, melted

Cut bread into very thin slices. Place on ungreased cookie sheet; brush bread with margarine. Bake at 325°, 10 to 12 minutes.

The clue to the lacy effect is very thin bread slices. An electric knife is a great slicing asset—so is a friendly baker who can cut the bread on a slicing machine. The bread will curl as it bakes. To make ahead, prepare and store in an airtight container; reheat at 350° or in microwave oven.

Scottish Scones

This oatmeal scone recipe emigrated from the Kraft Kitchens in Australia, and quickly found a new following—superb with honey spread.

1½ cups flour
¼ cup sugar
1 tablespoon baking powder
¾ teaspoon salt
¾ cup Parkay margarine

1½ cups old fashioned or quick oats, uncooked
⅓ cup chopped walnuts
⅓ cup milk

* * *

½ cup Parkay margarine
¼ cup honey

Combine dry ingredients; cut in margarine until mixture resembles coarse crumbs. Stir in oats and nuts. Add milk, mixing just until moistened. On lightly floured surface, roll dough to circle, ½ inch thick. Cut into ten wedges; place on greased cookie sheet. Bake at 425°, 12 to 15 minutes.

Cream margarine and honey until light and fluffy. Serve with warm scones. 10 scones

The Scots, English and Australians serve scones at teatime, accompanied by strawberry preserves and whipped cream. The English also serve Devonshire or Cornish cream, so richly thick it doesn't need to be whipped.

Pumpkin Bread

Moist, spicy and wonderfully fragrant, a family favorite.

1 16-oz. can pumpkin
1 cup Squeeze Parkay margarine
4 eggs, beaten
¼ cup water
3½ cups flour

3 cups sugar
4 teaspoons pumpkin pie spice
2 teaspoons soda
1½ teaspoons salt
1 cup chopped nuts

Combine pumpkin, margarine, eggs and water. Add combined dry ingredients except nuts; mix well. Stir in nuts. Pour into two greased and floured 9 × 5-inch loaf pans. Bake at 350°, 1 hour and 5 minutes. Cool 5 minutes; remove from pans. 2 loaves

Panettone

An Italian breakfast cake—originally a Christmas specialty.

5 to 5½ cups flour	¾ cup raisins
½ cup sugar	½ cup chopped citron
2 pkgs. active dry yeast	2 tablespoons chopped
1 teaspoon salt	walnuts
Parkay margarine	1 tablespoon anise seed
½ cup milk	* * *
½ cup water	1 egg, beaten
3 eggs	1 tablespoon water

In large mixing bowl, combine 1½ cups flour, sugar, yeast and salt. Heat ⅔ cup margarine, milk and water over low heat until warm. Add to flour mixture; beat 4 minutes on medium speed of electric mixer. Add 1 cup flour and eggs; beat 2 minutes at high speed. Stir in raisins, citron, nuts and anise seed. Stir in enough remaining flour to form a soft dough. On floured surface, knead dough until smooth and elastic. Place in greased bowl; brush with melted margarine. Cover; let rise in warm place until double in volume, about 1½ hours. Punch down dough. Cover; let rise about 30 minutes. Punch down dough; divide in half. Shape each half into round loaf; place on greased cookie sheet. Cut deep cross in top of each loaf. Cover; let rise about 1 hour.

Brush dough with combined egg and water. Bake at 350°, 35 to 40 minutes. 2 loaves

Parmesan Pan Rolls

Crisp, flavorful and extra-easy made with hot roll mix—these are marvelous pull-apart rolls.

1 13¾-oz. pkg. hot roll mix	¾ cup (3 ozs.) Kraft grated parmesan cheese
⅓ cup margarine, melted	

Prepare hot roll mix as directed on package. Cover; let rise in warm place until double in volume. Shape dough into sixteen balls. Dip in margarine; roll in cheese. Place in well-greased 9-inch layer pan. Cover; let rise until double in volume. Bake at 400°, 15 to 20 minutes. Remove from pan immediately. 16 rolls

Variation: Add ½ teaspoon dill weed to margarine.

Lemon Nut Bread

A citrus-flavored, fine-textured tea bread.

¾ cup Parkay margarine
1¼ cups sugar
3 eggs
2½ cups flour
2 teaspoons baking
powder

1 teaspoon salt
½ cup milk
⅓ cup lemon juice
¾ cup chopped pecans
2 teaspoons grated lemon
rind

Cream margarine and sugar until light and fluffy. Blend in eggs. Add combined dry ingredients to creamed mixture alternately with milk and juice, mixing well after each addition. Stir in nuts and rind. Pour into greased and floured 9 × 5-inch loaf pan. Bake at 350°, 1 hour and 20 minutes. Cool 5 minutes; remove from pan.

Variation: Substitute orange juice and rind for lemon.

Cheese Bread

This gorgeous golden loaf is a Kraft "classic" made with a classic cheese, cheddar. Serve it warm or toasted.

1 cup milk
2 tablespoons sugar
2 teaspoons salt
2 pkgs. active dry yeast
1½ cups warm water

5½ to 6 cups flour
2 cups (8 ozs.) shredded
Kraft sharp cheddar
cheese
Margarine, melted

Scald milk; stir in sugar and salt. Cool to lukewarm. Dissolve yeast in water; add milk mixture. Add 4 cups flour; mix well. Stir in cheese and enough remaining flour to form a soft dough. On floured surface, knead dough until smooth and elastic. Place in greased bowl; brush with margarine. Cover; let rise in warm place until double in volume. Punch down dough. On lightly floured surface, knead dough lightly; divide in half. Roll each half into a rectangle. Roll up from short side; press ends to seal. Fold ends under loaf; place seam-side down in greased 9 × 5-inch loaf pan. Cover; let rise until double in volume. Bake at 375°, 50 minutes. Remove from pan immediately.

Sally Lunn

English in origin, this recipe followed colonists to the south-eastern seaboard, and today is still a favorite throughout the South. High and fluted, this delicate-textured loaf is tender and mildly sweet.

4 cups flour	½ cup Parkay margarine
½ cup sugar	½ cup milk
1 pkg. active dry yeast	½ cup water
½ teaspoon salt	3 eggs

In large mixing bowl, combine 2 cups flour, sugar, yeast and salt. Heat margarine, milk and water over low heat until warm. Add to flour mixture; beat 2 minutes on medium speed of electric mixer. Blend in eggs; stir in remaining flour. Cover; let rise in warm place until double in volume, about 1 hour. Stir down dough; turn into well-greased and sugared 3-quart kugelhupf mold or 10-inch tube pan. Cover; let rise about 1 hour. Bake at 400°, 25 to 30 minutes. Cool 5 minutes; remove from pan. Serve warm.

Serve with fresh berries or melon, a cheese omelet and crisp bacon—perfect for Sunday brunch.

Cheddar Spoon Bread

This high-rising spectacular resembles a soufflé and should be treated with the same care—it should go directly from oven to table after guests are seated, before it begins to lose volume.

2 cups milk	¼ cup margarine
1 cup cornmeal	1 teaspoon salt
2 cups (8 ozs.) Kraft	Dash of cayenne
sharp cheddar cheese	4 eggs, separated

Heat milk. Gradually add cornmeal; cook, stirring constantly, until thickened and smooth. Remove from heat. Add cheese, margarine and seasonings. Gradually add slightly beaten egg yolks. Fold in stiffly beaten egg whites. Pour into greased 2-quart casserole. Bake at 375°, 35 to 40 minutes. Serve immediately.

Dainty Herb Crescents

Small and flavorful, these are frequently served in the dining room of the Kraft Kitchens with main-dish salads, chicken or soufflés.

1 8-oz. can refrigerated crescent rolls	Parkay margarine, melted Basil leaves, crushed

Separate dough into triangles. Cut each triangle in half lengthwise. Brush with margarine; sprinkle with basil. Roll up from wide end; form into crescent shape. Place on ungreased cookie sheet; brush with additional margarine. Bake at 375°, 10 to 12 minutes. 16 rolls

Variation: Substitute grated parmesan cheese for basil.

Crusty Cheese Bread

An easy favorite suitable for any casual occasion or family dinner, and an excellent choice for outdoor dining or campsite cooking.

French bread slices Margarine, melted	Kraft grated parmesan cheese

Brush one side of bread slices with margarine; sprinkle with cheese. Place on ungreased cookie sheet. Bake at 400°, 10 minutes.

Quick Cheddar Bread

For a weekend party, serve this crusty cheese loaf with egg, ham or chicken entrées and a crisp green salad.

3⅓ cups all purpose biscuit mix 2 cups (8 ozs.) shredded Kraft sharp cheddar cheese	1¼ cups milk 2 eggs, slightly beaten

Combine biscuit mix and cheese. Add milk and eggs, mixing just until moistened. Pour into greased and floured 9 × 5-inch loaf pan. Bake at 350°, 55 minutes. Remove from pan; serve warm.

Variation: Add ½ teaspoon dill weed.

The Kraft Story
1941–1945

Throughout World War II Kraft continued to produce products with high nutritive value for a low cost, serving families at home and the armed forces.

Although production plants remained in full operation, many products lost their familiar wrappings to reappear as Army and Navy rations. Tins and containers of all types bore simple labels such as "Kraft Cheese," "Kraft Salad Dressing," or "Kraft Ice Cream Mix." Kraft also developed new products to serve the war effort. Research scientists produced a spread for bread that would spread at temperatures of 5° below or 135° above zero. Another innovation was a one-ounce bar of dehydrated cheese with crackers.

On the home front, the National Defense Program sought to improve the nation's health by encouraging and educating the public to include the "protective foods" in the daily diet. Citing cheese as a concentrated form of important nutrients, the government appealed to dairymen and manufacturers for a tremendous increase in the production of this "protective food." Kraft responded by expanding its cooperative efforts with government agencies toward the improvement of dairying methods and by diverting more production plants to cheese making.

Homemakers throughout the country signed pledges to conserve food by using leftovers. To assist this effort, the Kraft Kitchens offered suggestions for "glamorizing" leftovers with cheese. Sauces, baked fondues, stratas, omelets, salads, and casseroles soon became popular everyday fare.

In 1945, after years of intensive research, a revolutionary method for producing Swiss cheese in 80-pound blocks was perfected. Traditionally Swiss cheese had been marketed in cumbersome 160 to 220-pound wheels. The new method improved the distribution of the characteristic Swiss "eyes" throughout the cheese. More importantly, the block was easier for grocers to handle, slice, pre-cut, and wrap, and the special protective wrapper eliminated rind and waste.

A major change in the company name also occurred in 1945. The Kraft Cheese Company became the Kraft Foods Company. The new name accurately reflected the product diversification that had been progressing over the past fifteen years and affirmed the continuance of this policy. By this time, products other than cheese represented fifty percent of the total volume.

Main Dishes

More than any other menu item, main dishes reflect the multinational origins of the American people. Throughout our history, immigrants from all parts of the world have settled here, bringing with them the culinary heritage of their native lands. Today our traditional cuisine has its roots in such diverse areas as Britain; Scandinavia; Africa; Europe; the Near, Middle, and Far East; Central and South America; Polynesia; and the Carribean.

Perhaps the major American contributions have been our abundant and varied food supply and the mingling of nationalities. The result has produced so many adaptations of the original dishes that a truly American cuisine emerged. For example, pizza in its original Italian form was a simple flat crust topped with tomato sauce, a few herbs, and possibly some sausage or anchovies. Pizza, American style, can have a thick or thin, soft or crisp crust covered with a mild or spicy sauce and just about any meat, seafood, vegetable, or cheese. A glance at the menu of most pizza parlors will reveal a minimum of ten selections.

Of course there are also many American originals such as baked ham, chicken à la king, meat loaf, Cornish hens, tuna casserole, barbecued ribs, and fried chicken.

The recipes that follow include a selection of tempting American or Americanized main dishes for family or guest dinners. Most are quick and simple and use everyday ingredients.

Florentine Spaghetti

In Italian cooking, "Florentine" indicates that there's spinach in the dish. This one layers spinach with a tangy spaghetti dinner, cottage cheese and mozzarella—great for an after-the-game crowd.

1 pkg. Kraft Italian spaghetti dinner	1 10-oz. pkg. frozen chopped spinach, partially thawed, drained
1 lb. ground beef	
1 6-oz. can tomato paste	
1½ cups water	1 8-oz. pkg. mozzarella cheese slices
1½ cups cottage cheese	

Prepare spaghetti as directed on package. Brown meat; drain. Stir in the herb-spice mix, tomato paste and water. Bring to boil; simmer 10 minutes. In 11¾ × 7½-inch baking dish, layer half of spaghetti, meat sauce, cottage cheese, spinach and mozzarella cheese; repeat layers. Sprinkle with the grated parmesan cheese. Bake at 350°, 25 minutes. 6 to 8 servings

Chuck Wagon Mac

This hearty skillet main dish combines savory meatballs with the ease and convenience of a packaged dinner.

1 lb. ground beef	1 7¼-oz. pkg. Kraft macaroni and cheese dinner
1 teaspoon salt	
Dash of pepper	
2 tablespoons oil	1 16-oz. can tomatoes
½ cup celery slices	1 12-oz. can whole kernel corn, drained
½ cup chopped onion	
¼ cup chopped green pepper	1 6-oz. can tomato paste

Combine meat and seasonings; mix lightly. Shape into twelve meatballs. In 12-inch skillet, brown meatballs in oil; drain. Add celery, onion and green pepper; cook until tender. Prepare dinner as directed on package. Add to meatballs with remaining ingredients; mix lightly. Simmer 15 minutes. 6 servings

This recipe was introduced to Kraft audiences in the early days of television and has never lost its popularity.

64

Epicurean Spaghetti

*A layered spaghetti lasagne with the appropriate Italian sea-
sonings and meat sauce, plus a marvelously creamy layer of
cream cheese, green pepper and onion.*

½ cup chopped green
   pepper
⅓ cup chopped onion
1 tablespoon margarine
1 8-oz. pkg. cream
   cheese, cubed

¼ cup milk
1 pkg. Kraft spaghetti
   with meat sauce
   dinner

Sauté vegetables in margarine. Add cream cheese and milk;
stir over low heat until smooth. Prepare spaghetti as directed
on package; combine with half of meat sauce. In 1½-quart
casserole, layer spaghetti mixture, cream cheese mixture and
remaining meat sauce; sprinkle with the grated parmesan
cheese. Bake at 350°, 30 minutes. 6 servings

Variation: Bake in a 10 × 6-inch baking dish.

To serve a crowd, double or triple the recipe as necessary,
serve with a crisp green salad, crusty Italian rolls and Mocha
Tortini.

Enchiladas

This south-of-the-border specialty is a great do-ahead dish.

1 lb. ground beef
1 16-oz. can tomatoes
1 6-oz. can tomato paste
½ cup water
½ cup chopped onion
1 tablespoon chili
   powder

1¼ teaspoons salt
¼ teaspoon pepper
1 8-oz. pkg. tortillas
Oil
2 cups (8 ozs.) shredded
   Kraft sharp cheddar
   cheese

Brown meat; drain. Add tomatoes, tomato paste, water,
onion and seasonings; simmer 10 minutes. Fry tortillas in hot
oil until softened; drain. Place rounded tablespoonful of meat
sauce and cheese on each tortilla; roll up tightly. Place seam
side down in 11¾ × 7½-inch baking dish; top with remaining
sauce and cheese. Cover with aluminum foil; bake at 375°, 25
minutes. 6 to 8 servings

To Make Ahead: Prepare recipe as directed. Cover; refrigerate overnight. Bake at 375°, 50 minutes.

Lasagne Italiano

Authentic Italian lasagne—a Kraft "classic" from the mid-1950s.

1 lb. ground beef
½ cup chopped onion
1 6-oz. can tomato paste
1½ cups water
1 garlic clove, minced
2 teaspoons salt
¾ teaspoon oregano
   leaves
¼ teaspoon pepper

8 ozs. lasagne noodles,
   cooked, drained
1 lb. ricotta or cottage
   cheese
2 6-oz. pkgs. Kraft
   mozzarella cheese
   slices
½ cup (2 ozs.) grated
   parmesan cheese

Brown meat; drain. Add onion; cook until tender. Stir in tomato paste, water and seasonings. Cover; simmer 30 minutes. In 11¾ × 7½-inch baking dish, layer half of noodles, meat sauce, ricotta cheese and mozzarella cheese; repeat layers. Sprinkle with parmesan cheese. Bake at 375°, 30 minutes. Let stand 10 minutes before serving. 6 to 8 servings

Stuffed Peppers

One of the first recipes advertised by Kraft in the 1920s. Here is an updated version featuring a modern sauce—Cheez Whiz process cheese spread.

6 medium green peppers
1 lb. ground beef
¼ cup chopped onion
2 cups hot cooked rice
1 8-oz. jar Cheez Whiz
   process cheese spread

Dash of pepper
Dash of basil
¼ cup dry bread crumbs
1 tablespoon margarine,
   melted

Remove tops and seeds from peppers. Parboil 5 minutes; drain. Brown meat; drain. Add onion; cook until tender. Stir in rice, cheese spread and seasonings; fill peppers. Place in baking dish; top with crumbs tossed with margarine. Bake at 350°, 40 minutes. 6 servings.

Lasagne

Kids love this updated version of an Italian classic in which Velveeta process cheese spread replaces ricotta.

1 lb. ground beef
½ cup chopped onion
1 16-oz. can tomatoes
1 6-oz. can tomato paste
⅓ cup water
1 garlic clove, minced
1 teaspoon oregano
    leaves
¼ teaspoon pepper

8 ozs. lasagne noodles,
    cooked, drained
2 6-oz. pkgs. mozzarella
    cheese slices
½ lb. Velveeta process
    cheese spread, thinly
    sliced
½ cup (2 ozs.) grated
    parmesan cheese

Brown meat; drain. Add onion; cook until tender. Stir in tomatoes, tomato paste, water and seasonings. Cover; simmer 30 minutes. In 11¾ × 7½-inch baking dish, layer half of noodles, meat sauce, mozzarella cheese, cheese spread and parmesan cheese; repeat layers. Bake at 350°, 30 minutes. Let stand 10 minutes before serving. 6 to 8 servings

Western Hash

A much-requested recipe, this flavorful ground beef dish appeared on television in the early 1950s and has been popular ever since.

1 lb. ground beef
1 28-oz. can tomatoes
1 cup rice
1 cup chopped green
    pepper
½ cup chopped onion

½ teaspoon salt
¼ teaspoon basil leaves,
    crushed
Dash of pepper
½ lb. Velveeta process
    cheese spread, sliced

Brown meat; drain. Add tomatoes, rice, green pepper, onion and seasonings; mix well. Cover; simmer 25 minutes. Top with cheese spread; cook until melted. 6 servings

Variation: Substitute 6 ounces shredded Kraft sharp cheddar cheese for Velveeta process cheese spread.

Barbecue Beef Pizza

A western-style pizza with a crisp homemade crust and a robust barbecue sauce combines with beef, sliced olives and two kinds of cheese to make it deliciously different.

1¾ cups flour	½ teaspoon salt
1 teaspoon baking powder	½ cup stuffed green olive slices
1 teaspoon salt	1 6-oz. pkg. mozzarella cheese slices, cut into strips
⅔ cup milk	
¼ cup oil	
* * *	Grated parmesan cheese
1 lb. ground beef	
¾ cup Kraft barbecue sauce	

Combine dry ingredients; add milk and oil. Stir with fork until mixture forms a ball. On lightly floured surface, knead dough ten times; roll out in 14-inch pizza pan.

Brown meat; drain. Combine meat, barbecue sauce and salt; spread on dough. Top with olives and mozzarella cheese; sprinkle with parmesan cheese. Bake at 425°, 20 minutes. 6 to 8 servings

Cheese 'n Frank Bake

Zesty barbecue sauce and a melted cheese topping make this traditional family favorite special.

¼ cup chopped green pepper	½ lb. frankfurters, sliced
¼ cup chopped onion	¼ cup barbecue sauce
2 tablespoons margarine	DeLuxe Choice process American cheese slices, cut in half diagonally
2 16-oz. cans pork and beans	

Sauté green pepper and onion in margarine. Stir in beans, frankfurters and barbecue sauce. Pour into 10 × 6-inch baking dish. Bake at 350°, 25 minutes. Top with cheese; continue baking until melted. 8 to 10 servings

Dad's Special

A favorite with Dad and the entire family—beef, noodles and cheddar cheese are always a winning combination.

1 lb. ground beef
½ cup chopped onion
1 10¾-oz. can condensed cream of mushroom soup
½ cup milk
½ teaspoon salt
¼ teaspoon thyme leaves, crushed
Dash of pepper
2 cups (4 ozs.) noodles, cooked, drained
2 cups (8 ozs.) shredded Kraft sharp cheddar cheese

Brown meat; drain. Add onion; cook until tender. Stir in soup, milk and seasonings. In 1½-quart casserole, layer half of noodles, meat mixture and cheese; repeat layers of noodles and meat mixture. Bake at 350°, 20 minutes. Top with remaining cheese; continue baking until melted. 4 to 6 servings

Mostaccioli

In the 1950s, Italian food gained widespread popularity, which has never waned. Mostaccioli made with Velveeta process cheese spread was Kraft's contribution to this ethnic cuisine.

½ lb. ground beef
½ cup chopped green pepper
½ cup chopped onion
1 16-oz. can tomatoes
1 6-oz. can tomato paste
½ cup water
1 bay leaf, crushed
½ teaspoon salt
¼ teaspoon pepper
8 ozs. mostaccioli noodles, cooked, drained
½ lb. Velveeta process cheese spread, thinly sliced
Grated parmesan cheese

Brown meat; drain. Add green pepper and onion; cook until tender. Stir in tomatoes, tomato paste, water and seasonings. In 11¾ × 7½-inch baking dish, layer half of noodles, meat sauce and cheese spread; repeat layers of noodles and meat sauce. Bake at 350°, 30 minutes. Top with remaining cheese spread; sprinkle with parmesan cheese. Continue baking until cheese spread is melted. 6 to 8 servings

Potatoes and Frankfurters Au Gratin

A great one-dish meal that combines franks, potatoes and vegetables in a creamy, delectable cheese sauce.

2 tablespoons margarine
¼ cup flour
1 cup milk
¼ teaspoon salt
Dash of pepper
½ lb. Velveeta process cheese spread, cubed

4 cups chopped cooked potatoes
1 lb. frankfurters, cut into 1-inch pieces
1 10-oz. pkg. frozen peas and carrots, cooked, drained

Make a white sauce with margarine, flour, milk and seasonings. Add cheese spread; stir until melted. Add remaining ingredients; mix well. Spoon into 2-quart casserole. Bake at 350°, 1 hour. 6 to 8 servings

Velveeta process cheese spread has been a family staple since it was first introduced in 1928 as a mild, nutritious cheese spread with special appeal for children. Homemakers soon learned that it was not only great for sandwiches and snacks, but quickly melted into a smooth, flavorful sauce for vegetables, casseroles and main dishes.

Rhineland Supper

Sour cream, dill pickle and bratwurst add Bavarian flavor to an old favorite—macaroni and cheese.

2 pkgs. Kraft macaroni and cheese deluxe dinner
1 cup dairy sour cream
½ cup chopped dill pickles

½ cup green onion slices
1 tablespoon prepared mustard
8 bratwurst, cooked

Prepare dinner as directed on package. Add remaining ingredients except bratwurst; mix lightly. Heat thoroughly. Serve with bratwurst. 8 servings

For informal entertaining, serve Rhineland Supper with a spinach salad, pumpernickel or rye bread, and Heidelberg Chocolate Cake.

Spanish Pot Roast

Catalina French dressing adds a zesty flavor to pot roast.

3 to 4-lb. pot roast
1 8-oz. bottle Catalina
  French dressing
¾ cup water
8 small onions

8 small potatoes
1 cup stuffed green olive
  slices
2 tablespoons flour

Brown meat in ¼ cup dressing. Add remaining dressing and ½ cup water. Cover; simmer 2 hours and 15 minutes. Add onions, potatoes and olives; continue simmering 45 minutes or until meat and vegetables are tender. Remove meat and vegetables to serving platter. Gradually add remaining water to flour, stirring until well blended. Gradually add flour mixture to hot liquid in pan; cook, stirring constantly, until mixture boils and thickens. Simmer 3 minutes, stirring constantly. Serve with meat and vegetables. 6 to 8 servings

This pot roast was demonstrated on Kraft's first "omnibus" 90-second commercial, which featured a range of recipes from appetizer to dessert—a complete meal. It was a Kraft first, and an extra service to our viewers.

Ribs Ranchero

At home or at a cookout, these barbecued spareribs are great for a crowd—orange slices brushed with the tangy sauce add an attractive touch and a refreshing, mild citrus flavor.

Spareribs
Kraft barbecue sauce

Orange slices

Indoor Method: Place ribs on rack of broiler pan. Brush with barbecue sauce. Bake at 350°, 1 hour and 30 minutes, turning and brushing with barbecue sauce every 15 minutes. Brush orange slices with barbecue sauce; bake with ribs last 15 minutes.

Outdoor Method: Place ribs on greased grill, bone side down, 5 to 7 inches from coals. Grill over low coals (coals will be ash gray) 30 minutes. Turn; grill additional 45 minutes, turning and brushing with barbecue sauce every 10 minutes. Brush orange slices with barbecue sauce; grill last 10 minutes.

Cheddar Top Meat Loaf

Meat loaf again? Turn it into something special for a family or company dinner with barbecue sauce and cheddar cheese.

2 lbs. ground beef
2 cups soft bread crumbs
1½ cups (6 ozs.) shredded
   Kraft sharp cheddar
   cheese
¾ cup barbecue sauce

½ cup chopped celery
½ cup chopped onion
1 egg
1 teaspoon salt
¼ teaspoon pepper

Combine meat, crumbs, 1 cup cheese, ½ cup barbecue sauce and remaining ingredients; mix lightly. Shape into round loaf in shallow baking dish. Bake at 350°, 45 minutes. Brush with remaining barbecue sauce; continue baking 15 minutes. Top with remaining cheese. 8 servings

Barbecued Short Ribs

No seasoning is needed, other than the expert blend of herbs and spices in the barbecue sauce.

4½ lbs. beef short ribs
2 tablespoons oil
2 cups Kraft barbecue
   sauce

1½ cups water
1 large green pepper, cut
   into rings
1 large onion, sliced

In Dutch oven, brown meat in oil; drain. Add remaining ingredients; bring to boil. Cover; bake at 350°, 1 hour and 30 minutes or until meat is tender. Skim off fat. Thicken gravy, if desired. 8 servings

Stroganoff Superb

If you've never made stroganoff with cream cheese, start now!

1 lb. round steak, cut
   into thin strips
3 tablespoons margarine
½ cup chopped onion
1 4-oz. can mushrooms,
   drained
½ teaspoon salt

¼ teaspoon dry mustard
¼ teaspoon pepper
1 8-oz. pkg. Philadelphia
   Brand cream cheese,
   cubed
¾ cup milk
Hot parslied noodles

Brown meat in margarine. Add onion, mushrooms and seasonings; cook 5 minutes or until tender. Add cream cheese and milk; stir over low heat until smooth. Serve over noodles. 4 to 6 servings

Beef Fondue

To entertain with flair and ease, serve beef fondue with a choice of several sauces. This sophisticated entrée is especially designed for intimate dinner parties and after-theater gatherings.

Oil   Mustard Sauce
2 lbs. beef sirloin, cut   India Sauce
   into 1-inch cubes   Sauce Piquant
Grated parmesan
   cheese

Pour oil into fondue pot to 2-inch depth; heat to 375°. Spear meat with fondue fork. Place in hot oil; cook to desired doneness. Serve with parmesan cheese and any of following sauces:

Mustard Sauce

¾ cup Kraft real   2 tablespoons
   mayonnaise   prepared mustard

Combine ingredients; mix well.

India Sauce

½ cup Kraft real   1 tablespoon green onion
   mayonnaise   slices
½ cup dairy sour cream   1 teaspoon curry powder
1 tablespoon milk

Combine ingredients; mix well.

Sauce Piquant

1 cup chili sauce   ¼ cup Kraft cream
                 style horseradish

Combine ingredients; mix well. 6 to 8 servings

In 1942, Kraft Music Hall (with Bing Crosby) shared top-favorite radio program honors with such celebrities as Fibber McGee and Molly, Jack Benny, Edgar Bergen and Charlie McCarthy, Bob Hope and Kate Smith.

Rinderrouladen

A specialty from the Kraft Kitchens in Germany, unique steak roll-ups braised in tangy Catalina French dressing that flavors and tenderizes the meat as it cooks—an excellent recipe for a slow cooker.

2 lbs. lean, boneless
round steak,
½ inch thick
12 carrot sticks
6 dill pickle spears

¾ cup Catalina French
dressing
1¼ cups water
1 medium onion, sliced

Cut meat into six pieces. For each serving, wrap one piece of meat around two carrot sticks and one pickle spear; secure with picks. Brown in ½ cup dressing. Add remaining dressing, water and onion; bring to boil. Cover; simmer 1 hour or until meat is tender. Thicken gravy, if desired. 6 servings

To Make in Slow Cooker: Prepare roll-ups as directed. Place roll-ups, dressing, water and onion in slow cooker. Cover; cook on high setting 4 hours or low setting 8 hours. Thicken gravy, if desired.

Golden Glazed Ham

This gorgeously glazed ham does justice to any occasion.

4 to 5-lb. canned ham
1 10-oz. jar Kraft orange
marmalade
½ cup orange juice
1 tablespoon prepared
mustard

¼ teaspoon ground cloves
¼ teaspoon ginger
Whole cloves
½ cup raisins

Place ham, fat side up, on rack in baking pan; score fat. Bake at 325°, 1 hour and 15 minutes. Combine marmalade, orange juice, mustard, ground cloves and ginger; simmer 5 minutes. Spoon half of marmalade mixture over ham; stud with whole cloves. Continue baking 30 minutes. Combine remaining marmalade mixture and raisins; serve with ham. 10 to 12 servings

Southern-Style Sweet Potatoes and Cranberry Nut Bread are perfect partners for this superb ham.

Harlequin Ham Casserole

This colorful Kraft "classic" is an excellent encore for left-over ham and rice. Miracle Whip salad dressing provides the seasoning, as well as the base for the extra-creamy sauce.

⅓ cup Miracle Whip
   salad dressing
3 tablespoons flour
1 cup milk
2 cups ham cubes
2 cups cooked rice
½ cup chopped green
   pepper

1 6-oz. can water
   chestnuts, drained,
   sliced
⅓ cup grated parmesan
   cheese
¼ cup chopped pimiento

Combine salad dressing and flour; gradually add milk. Cook over low heat, stirring constantly, until thickened. Add remaining ingredients; mix well. Spoon into 1½-quart casserole. Cover; bake at 350°, 40 minutes. 4 to 6 servings

Grenoble Goulash

Very continental—Hungarian pork stew with a tangy Italian sauce. This spaghetti goulash is a great favorite with the Kraft Kitchens staff.

1 lb. boneless pork
   shoulder, cut into
   ½-inch cubes
¼ cup margarine
½ cup chopped onion
1 pkg. Kraft Italian
   spaghetti dinner

1 16-oz. can tomatoes
1 6-oz. can tomato paste
¾ cup water
4 large carrots
1 cup celery slices

Brown meat in 2 tablespoons margarine. Add onion; cook until tender. Stir in the herb-spice mix, tomatoes, tomato paste and water. Cover; simmer 20 minutes. Cut carrots in half lengthwise, then into ½-inch pieces. Add to meat mixture with celery. Cover; continue simmering 10 to 15 minutes or until vegetables are tender. Prepare spaghetti as directed on package. Stir in remaining margarine and the grated parmesan cheese; mix lightly. Serve meat mixture over spaghetti. 6 to 8 servings

Homesteader's Casserole

A midwestern sausage dish, sauced with smooth-melting Velveeta process cheese spread.

1 9-oz. pkg. frozen cut green beans, cooked, drained
1 8-oz. can small whole onions, drained
1 tablespoon chopped pimiento
3 cups hot mashed potatoes
1 lb. pork sausage links, cooked, drained
½ lb. Velveeta process cheese spread, sliced

Combine green beans, onions and pimiento. In 2-quart casserole, layer half the potatoes, sausage and cheese spread; top with remaining potatoes, green bean mixture, remaining sausage and cheese spread. Cover; bake at 350°, 30 minutes. 4 to 6 servings

Savory Sausage Noodle Pie

Attractive and nutritious, this features a unique use of a convenience dinner—as a pie shell for a savory sausage filling.

1 pkg. Kraft egg noodle and cheese dinner
1 egg, beaten
1 lb. bulk pork sausage
1½ cups zucchini slices
1 6-oz. can tomato paste
¼ cup water
½ teaspoon oregano leaves, crushed

Prepare dinner as directed on package, omitting milk. Add egg; mix well. Press noodle mixture onto bottom and sides of 9-inch pie plate. Brown meat; drain. Add zucchini; cook until crisp-tender. Stir in tomato paste, water and oregano; spoon into noodle shell. Bake at 350°, 30 minutes. Let stand 5 minutes before serving. 6 servings

In 1941, Kraft launched a new weekly radio comedy which featured Throckmorton P. Gildersleeve — the "Great Gildersleeve" — and remained a popular program for more than a decade.

Bacon-Spinach Bake

Decidedly different and definitely delicious, this baked cheese and noodle custard is a complete meal for lunch or supper.

1 pkg. Kraft egg noodle
  and cheese dinner
1 10-oz. pkg. frozen
  chopped spinach,
  partially thawed
6 crisply cooked bacon
  slices, crumbled

2 eggs, beaten
¼ teaspoon salt
  Dash of pepper
2 cups bread cubes
2 tablespoons margarine,
  melted

Prepare dinner as directed on package, except using ¾ cup milk. Add spinach, bacon, eggs and seasonings; mix well. Pour into 8-inch square baking dish. Top with bread cubes tossed with margarine. Bake at 350°, 30 minutes. Let stand 5 minutes before serving. 6 servings

To accompany the dinner, serve marinated tomatoes and Rye Lace.

Green Noodle and Ham Casserole

A holiday dish based on leftover ham or turkey in a tangy cheese sauce. If you've never had green noodles (spinach gives them their lovely flavor and color), you're in for a treat.

2 tablespoons chopped
  onion
  Margarine
1 tablespoon flour
½ teaspoon salt
  Dash of pepper
1¼ cups milk
1 cup (4 ozs.) shredded
  Kraft sharp cheddar
  cheese

1 cup ham cubes
1 4-oz. can mushrooms,
  drained
2 cups (4 ozs.) green
  noodles, cooked,
  drained
½ cup dry bread crumbs

Sauté onion in 1 tablespoon margarine until tender. Blend in flour and seasonings; gradually add milk. Cook, stirring constantly, until thickened. Add cheese, ham and mushrooms; stir until cheese is melted. In 10 × 6-inch baking dish, layer half of noodles and sauce; repeat layers. Top with crumbs tossed with 2 tablespoons melted margarine. Bake at 350°, 30 minutes. 6 servings

Fireside Supper

It's amazing what macaroni and cheese can do for leftover ham or turkey—the perfect dish for unexpected guests. Sour cream and a choice herb or two add a touch of elegance.

1 7¼-oz. pkg. Kraft macaroni and cheese dinner
2 cups chopped cooked ham, turkey or chicken
1 10-oz. pkg. frozen peas and carrots, cooked, drained

1 cup dairy sour cream
¼ cup chopped onion
1 tablespoon chopped parsley
¼ teaspoon rosemary
Dash of pepper

Prepare dinner as directed on package. Add remaining ingredients; mix well. Heat thoroughly, stirring occasionally. 6 servings

Baked Chicken Salad

Something different for family and guests—a hot, creamy chicken salad topped with crispy chips and fresh tomatoes.

3 cups chopped cooked chicken
1½ cups celery slices
1 cup (4 ozs.) shredded Kraft sharp cheddar cheese
1 tablespoon chopped onion

1 tablespoon lemon juice
1½ teaspoons salt
Dash of pepper
Mayonnaise
Tomato slices
1½ cups crushed potato chips

Combine chicken, celery, ½ cup cheese, onion, lemon juice, seasonings and enough mayonnaise to moisten; mix lightly. Spoon into 1½-quart casserole; top with tomatoes. Bake at 350°, 35 minutes. Top with combined remaining cheese and chips; continue baking until cheese is melted. 6 servings

Baked Chicken Salad→

Alpine Chicken Casserole

A do-ahead dish for easy entertaining. Prepare the day before and refrigerate until time to bake. Leftover turkey can substitute for chicken.

4 cups chopped cooked chicken
2 cups celery slices
2 cups toasted bread cubes
1 cup salad dressing or mayonnaise
½ cup milk
¼ cup chopped onion
1 teaspoon salt
Dash of pepper
1 8-oz. pkg. Kraft Swiss cheese slices, cut into thin strips
¼ cup slivered almonds, toasted

Combine ingredients except nuts; mix well. Pour into 2-quart casserole; sprinkle with nuts. Bake at 350°, 40 minutes. 6 servings

To Make Ahead: Prepare the recipe as directed. Cover; refrigerate several hours. Bake at 350°, 50 minutes. Uncover; continue baking 10 minutes.

Cheddar Chicken

Herb-seasoned chicken breasts with a rich cheddar topping —easy and elegant for entertaining, served with Herb Rice.

4 chicken breasts, split, skinned
⅓ cup margarine, melted
1 teaspoon basil leaves
½ teaspoon salt
¼ teaspoon pepper
1 cup (4 ozs.) shredded Kraft sharp cheddar cheese
1 tablespoon chopped parsley

Brush chicken with combined margarine and seasonings. Place in baking dish. Bake at 350°, 50 minutes, basting occasionally. Combine cheese and parsley; sprinkle over chicken. Continue baking 10 minutes. 8 servings

Simmer the leftover chicken skins in lightly salted water to make a broth for future use in sauces, soups or casseroles.

Canton Chicken

Preserves or marmalade blended with soy sauce and sherry provides a delicious sweet-sour sauce.

2½ to 3-lb. broiler-fryer, cut up
1 10-oz. jar Kraft apricot preserves or orange marmalade

¼ cup soy sauce
¼ cup sherry
¼ cup finely chopped onion

Place chicken in 11¾ × 7½-inch baking dish. Combine remaining ingredients; pour over chicken. Bake at 325°, 1 hour, turning occasionally. Thicken sauce, if desired. 3 servings

Canton Chicken served with fluffy rice and a tossed salad of mixed greens makes a dinner worthy of any occasion.

Chicken à la King

A Kraft "classic" and a national institution in the 1920s and '30s. Served in patty shells, this was an elegant "must" for all occasions, from ladies' luncheons to formal banquets.

½ cup Miracle Whip salad dressing
¼ cup flour
2 cups milk
¼ cup chopped pimiento
2 tablespoons finely chopped onion

¼ teaspoon salt
⅛ teaspoon pepper
2 cups chopped cooked chicken or turkey
1 4-oz. can mushrooms, drained

Combine salad dressing and flour; gradually add milk. Add pimiento, onion and seasonings; cook over low heat, stirring constantly, until thickened. Add chicken and mushrooms; continue cooking 5 minutes. Serve over hot cooked rice, toast or toasted English muffins. 6 servings

Variation: Substitute 2 cups ham cubes or two 6½-oz. cans tuna, drained, for the chicken.

Chicken Rococo

The Kraft Kitchen's elegant version of Chicken Kiev. You can bone the chicken breasts with a very sharp knife or have it done at the market.

1 10-oz. stick Cracker
Barrel sharp cheddar
cheese
4 chicken breasts, split,
boned, skinned

2 eggs, beaten
¾ cup dry bread crumbs
Margarine

Cut cheese into eight equal sticks. Flatten chicken breasts to ¼-inch thickness. Roll each piece around stick of cheese; secure with picks. Dip in eggs; coat with crumbs. Brown in margarine on all sides; place in baking dish. Bake at 400°, 20 minutes. 8 servings

For a fine balance of flavors and textures, serve this superb chicken dish with wild rice or brown rice, a fresh fruit salad and, for dessert, Grasshopper Torte.

Chow Mein Casserole

A marvelous blend of flavors—soy sauce, cheddar, mushrooms and water chestnuts—this Kraft "classic" has appeared frequently in our television commercials and is distinctive enough for any occasion.

2 tablespoons margarine
2 tablespoons flour
1½ cups milk
1 teaspoon soy sauce
½ teaspoon salt
¼ teaspoon pepper
2 cups (8 ozs.) shredded
Kraft sharp cheddar
cheese
2 cups cooked rice

2 cups chopped cooked
chicken
1 6-oz. can water
chestnuts, drained,
sliced
1 4-oz. can mushrooms,
drained
1 3-oz. can chow mein
noodles

Make a white sauce with margarine, flour, milk and seasonings. Add cheese; stir until melted. Combine rice, chicken, water chestnuts and mushrooms; mix lightly. In 2-quart casserole, layer half of rice mixture and cheese sauce; repeat layers. Top with noodles. Bake at 350°, 35 minutes. 6 to 8 servings

Country Cornish Hens

These succulent birds, dressed with a southern sausage stuffing, are perfect for buffet dining. Garnish with celery leaves and orange twists.

½ lb. bulk pork sausage
2 cups bread cubes, toasted
1 cup chopped peeled apple
½ cup celery slices
⅓ cup raisins
⅓ cup chopped onion

¾ cup Parkay margarine, melted
⅓ cup sherry
¼ teaspoon sage
¼ teaspoon salt
Dash of pepper
6 1 to 1½-lb. Rock Cornish hens

Brown meat; drain. Add bread, apple, celery, raisins, onion, ¼ cup margarine, 2 tablespoons sherry and seasonings. Lightly stuff hens with dressing; close openings with skewers. Bake at 400°, 1 hour or until tender, basting occasionally with combined remaining margarine and sherry. 6 servings

To complete the main course, serve Cranberry Crimson Mold and Dainty Herb Crescents.

Creamy Chicken Casserole

A down-home, one-dish dinner, delicately seasoned with mayonnaise and topped with crisp corn flakes—bread crumbs or crunchy croutons, if you prefer.

2 cups chopped cooked chicken or turkey
1½ cups hot cooked rice
1 10¾-oz. can condensed cream of mushroom soup
¾ cup Kraft real mayonnaise

3 hard-cooked eggs, chopped
¼ cup finely chopped onion
½ teaspoon salt
1 cup corn flakes
1 tablespoon margarine, melted

Combine chicken, rice, soup, mayonnaise, eggs, onion and salt; mix well. Pour into 1½-quart casserole. Top with corn flakes tossed with margarine. Bake at 375°, 45 minutes. 4 to 6 servings

Irish Soda Bread and green beans go well with this casserole.

Oven-Fried Chicken Parmesan

This all-American chicken has the added convenience of oven-frying, making it ideal for family reunions or similar celebrations. Increase the recipe as required to serve a crowd of almost any size.

½ cup (2 ozs.) Kraft
   grated parmesan
   cheese
¼ cup flour
1 teaspoon paprika
½ teaspoon salt
   Dash of pepper

2½ to 3-lb. broiler-fryer,
   cut up
1 egg, slightly beaten
1 tablespoon milk
¼ cup Squeeze Parkay
   margarine

Combine cheese, flour and seasonings. Dip chicken in combined egg and milk; coat with cheese mixture. Place in baking dish; pour margarine over chicken. Bake at 350°, 1 hour or until tender. 3 to 4 servings

Jamaican Chicken

This exceptional entrée features the unlikely combination of chicken, cheddar cheese, coffee and pineapple—with great success.

6 pineapple slices
3 chicken breasts, split
   Salt and pepper
1 10¾-oz. can condensed
   cream of chicken soup

1 teaspoon instant coffee
1 cup (4 ozs.) shredded
   Kraft sharp cheddar
   cheese

Place pineapple slices in 11¾ × 7½-inch baking dish; top with chicken breasts. Season with salt and pepper. Combine soup and coffee; spoon over chicken. Bake at 375°, 40 minutes. Top with cheese; bake until melted. 6 servings

To complete the meal, serve parslied rice and broccoli, with lemon sherbet for dessert.

Creamy Spoleto Spaghetti

Tangy Italian spaghetti without tomato—the herb-spice mix seasons the sauce. Also try it with seafood, such as shrimp. Superb!

1 cup green pepper strips	2 tablespoons flour
¼ cup margarine, melted	2 cups milk
1 pkg. Kraft Italian spaghetti dinner	2 cups chopped cooked chicken or turkey

Sauté green pepper in margarine. Blend in the herb-spice mix and flour. Gradually add milk; cook, stirring constantly, until thickened. Add chicken. Cover; simmer 10 minutes. Prepare spaghetti as directed on package. Pour sauce over spaghetti; sprinkle with the grated parmesan cheese. 4 to 6 servings

Variation: Substitute 1 cup sliced mushrooms, zucchini or celery for green pepper.

For accompaniment, serve heated Italian bread, marinated tomato slices and Swiss Chocolate Squares.

Poulet Français

Chicken and blue cheese combine in an epicurean dish for family or entertaining. Recipe can be doubled or tripled as necessary.

2½ to 3-lb. broiler-fryer, cut up	¾ cup Roka blue cheese dressing
¼ cup flour	
Dash of salt and pepper	

Coat chicken with combined flour and seasonings; dip in dressing. Place in baking dish. Bake at 350°, 50 to 60 minutes or until tender. 4 servings

Complete the menu with fresh asparagus and Marshmallow Waldorf Salad.

Turkey Tetrazzini

Another Kraft "classic"—tetrazzini made with Miracle Whip salad dressing and topped with crunchy parmesan croutons.

⅔ cup Miracle Whip salad dressing
⅓ cup flour
½ teaspoon salt
Dash of pepper
2½ cups milk
7 ozs. spaghetti, cooked, drained
2 cups chopped cooked turkey

¾ cup grated parmesan cheese
1 4-oz. can mushrooms, drained
2 tablespoons chopped pimiento
2 cups bread cubes
¼ cup Squeeze Parkay margarine

Combine salad dressing, flour and seasonings; gradually add milk. Cook over low heat, stirring constantly, until thickened. Add spaghetti, turkey, ½ cup cheese, mushrooms and pimiento; mix lightly. Pour into 2-quart casserole. Top with bread cubes tossed with margarine and remaining cheese. Bake at 350°, 40 minutes. 6 servings

Big Catch Casserole

A complete one-dish fish dinner with peas and noodles. Miracle Whip salad dressing provides the seasonings and the creamy texture.

1 10¾-oz. can condensed cream of celery soup
½ cup Miracle Whip salad dressing
¼ cup milk
¼ cup (1 oz.) grated parmesan cheese
1 16-oz. can salmon, drained, flaked

1 10-oz. pkg. frozen peas, cooked, drained
2 cups (4 ozs.) noodles, cooked, drained
1 tablespoon chopped onion

Combine soup, salad dressing, milk and cheese; mix well. Add remaining ingredients; mix lightly. Pour into 1½-quart casserole. Cover; bake at 350°, 45 minutes. 6 to 8 servings

Fish à la Maison

Perch, trout, haddock or cod, or any white fish fillets are enhanced by this crisp parmesan coating.

1 lb. fish fillets
1 egg, slightly beaten
1 tablespoon milk
1 cup dry bread crumbs

⅓ cup Kraft grated
  parmesan cheese
Squeeze Parkay
  margarine

Dip fillets in combined egg and milk; coat with combined crumbs and cheese. Fry in margarine until golden brown on both sides. 4 servings

Variation: Add 1 tablespoon finely chopped parsley or ½ teaspoon basil leaves to crumb mixture.

Fish cooked this way is delicious with Tartar Sauce or Royal Mustard Sauce.

Clam Digger Dinner

Clams and spaghetti, a favorite combination of shellfish lovers.

1 pkg. Kraft Italian
  spaghetti dinner
1 8-oz. can minced clams,
  drained

2 tablespoons sherry
2 tablespoons chopped
  parsley

Prepare spaghetti and sauce as directed on package. Add clams and sherry to sauce; heat thoroughly. Serve over spaghetti. Sprinkle with parsley and the grated parmesan cheese. 4 servings

Variations: Omit sherry. Substitute 2 cups cooked shrimp for clams. Add ½ cup mushroom slices, onion rings or chopped green pepper to sauce.

Serve with Mushroom Bread and Spinach Salad, with cheese and fresh fruit for dessert.

Introduced in 1945, Kraft grated parmesan cheese in the handy shaker container is now a staple in many homes. Sprinkle grated parmesan cheese on salads, soups, hot breads, broiled meat patties, casseroles or almost any pasta dish.

Pacific Salmon Loaf

Salmon, cucumber and dill combine in a refreshing fish dish for any season—a long-time favorite with our television viewers.

1 16-oz. can salmon, drained, flaked
½ cup dry bread crumbs
½ cup Kraft real mayonnaise
½ cup chopped onion
¼ cup chopped celery
¼ cup chopped green pepper
1 egg, beaten
1 teaspoon salt
Cucumber Sauce

Combine ingredients except Cucumber Sauce; mix lightly. Shape into loaf in shallow baking dish. Bake at 350°, 40 minutes. Serve with:

Cucumber Sauce

½ cup Kraft real mayonnaise
½ cup dairy sour cream
½ cup finely chopped cucumber
2 tablespoons chopped onion
½ teaspoon dill weed

Combine ingredients; mix well. 6 to 8 servings

Variation: Substitute two 6½-oz. cans tuna for salmon.

San Lorenzo Shrimp

This savory shrimp entrée bears a marked resemblance to shrimp de jonghe. Don't overcook the shrimp—just a few minutes in boiling water is enough.

½ cup Parkay margarine
½ cup (2 ozs.) grated parmesan cheese
½ cup dry bread crumbs
⅓ cup chopped onion
2 tablespoons lemon juice
1 garlic clove, minced
¼ teaspoon salt
1½ lbs. frozen cleaned shrimp, cooked, drained

Combine ingredients except shrimp; mix well. Add shrimp; mix lightly. Spoon mixture into 1-quart casserole. Bake at 350°, 35 minutes. 6 servings

Souffléed Salmon Steaks

Arranged on a handsome platter, garnished with lemon slices and parsley, these salmon steaks with souffléed topping are a dramatic attraction when you want to serve guests something very special.

¼ cup margarine, melted
2 tablespoons dry white
    wine
6 (2 lbs.) salmon steaks,
    1 inch thick
3 egg whites

½ cup Kraft real
    mayonnaise
2 tablespoons green
    onion slices
½ teaspoon dry mustard

Combine margarine and wine. Place fish on greased rack of broiler pan. Broil 6 to 8 minutes on each side until fish flakes easily with fork, brushing frequently with margarine mixture. Beat egg whites until stiff peaks form; fold in mayonnaise, onion and mustard. Spoon onto fish; broil until lightly browned. 6 servings

Variation: Halibut steaks can be substituted for salmon.

Stuffed Fish

Spectacular dish for guests or special family occasions—garnish the fish with lemon twists and sprigs of curly endive or parsley.

½ cup chopped celery
½ cup mushroom slices
¼ cup green onion slices
    Parkay margarine
2 cups cooked rice
½ teaspoon poultry
    seasoning

¼ teaspoon salt
    Dash of pepper
1 egg, beaten
3 to 4-lb. white fish,
    pan-dressed

Sauté vegetables in ¼ cup margarine. Add rice and seasonings; mix well. Stir in egg. Stuff fish with rice mixture; close opening with skewers or picks. Place in large well-greased baking dish; brush with melted margarine. Bake at 350°, 45 minutes or until fish flakes easily with fork. 6 to 8 servings

The rice stuffing can be prepared in advance and refrigerated.

Creamy Tuna Casserole

Favorite tuna casseroles are extra easy when you start with a convenience dinner and add imaginative ingredients such as ripe olives, sour cream and parsley.

1 pkg. Kraft macaroni and cheese deluxe dinner	½ cup chopped onion
1 cup dairy sour cream	¼ cup pitted ripe olive slices
1 6½-oz. can tuna, drained, flaked	2 tablespoons chopped parsley
	¼ teaspoon pepper

Prepare dinner as directed on package. Add remaining ingredients; mix well. Pour into 10 × 6-inch baking dish. Cover with aluminum foil; bake at 350°, 25 minutes. 6 servings

To Make Ahead: Prepare recipe as directed. Cover; refrigerate. Bake at 350°, 1 hour and 20 minutes.

Kraft macaroni and cheese dinner was a regular dinner feature for "meatless Tuesdays," a weekly event with patriotic Americans. Kraft macaroni and cheese deluxe dinner was a later addition to the convenience dinner line.

Jiffy Tuna Soufflé

This hearty dish is a cross between a casserole and a soufflé.

1 10¾-oz. can condensed cream of celery soup	¾ cup hot cooked rice
1 cup (4 ozs.) shredded Kraft sharp cheddar cheese	2 tablespoons chopped pimiento
	Dash of pepper
1 6½-oz. can tuna, drained, flaked	3 eggs, separated

Heat soup. Add cheese; stir until melted. Remove from heat. Stir in tuna, rice, pimiento and pepper. Gradually add slightly beaten egg yolks; cool. Fold in stiffly beaten egg whites; pour into 10 × 6-inch baking dish. Bake at 325°, 50 minutes. Serve immediately. 6 servings

Serve Jiffy Tuna Soufflé with Rye Lace and a mixed green salad.

Oriental Tuna Casserole

One of the first dishes to feature Miracle Whip salad dressing as a sauce for casseroles and main dishes. This recipe appeared on television in the late 1950s.

1 cup Miracle Whip
    salad dressing
⅓ cup flour
2 cups milk
1 10-oz. pkg. frozen peas,
    cooked, drained

1 6½-oz. can tuna,
    drained, flaked
2 tablespoons chopped
    onion
1 6-oz. can chow mein
    noodles

Combine salad dressing and flour; gradually add milk. Cook over low heat, stirring constantly, until thickened. Add peas, tuna and onion; mix lightly. Place half of noodles on bottom of 1½-quart casserole; top with tuna mixture and remaining noodles. Bake at 350°, 25 minutes. 4 to 6 servings

Tasty Tuna Turnover

This luncheon favorite makes a nice change from routine tuna salad sandwiches.

1 6½-oz. can tuna,
    drained, flaked
2 tablespoons sweet
    pickle relish, drained
¼ teaspoon pepper
    Mayonnaise

1 8-oz. can refrigerated
    crescent rolls
1 8-oz. pkg. Kraft sharp
    cheddar cheese slices,
    cut in half

Combine tuna, relish, pepper and enough mayonnaise to moisten; mix lightly. Separate dough into four rectangles; firmly press perforations to seal. On floured surface, roll out dough to 8 × 5-inch rectangles. For each turnover, cover half of dough with cheese slice, ¼ cup tuna mixture and second cheese slice. Fold dough over filling. Moisten edges; seal with fork. Prick tops; place on ungreased cookie sheet. Bake at 375°, 18 to 20 minutes. 4 servings

To serve, cut diagonally in half and garnish with ripe olives.

Tunamato Dinner

Quick, easy and so good—a supper dish to please the whole family.

1 7¼-oz. pkg. Kraft
  macaroni and cheese
  dinner
2 tablespoons chopped
  onion
2 tablespoons margarine

1 16-oz. can tomatoes,
  drained
1 6½-oz. can tuna,
  drained, flaked
2 tablespoons chopped
  parsley
¼ teaspoon salt

Prepare dinner as directed on package. Sauté onion in margarine. Add to dinner with remaining ingredients; heat thoroughly. 4 servings

Although Kraft marketed its first macaroni and cheese product in 1922, the present version was introduced in 1936. It was an immediate success, and its popularity has steadily increased through the years. "Mac and cheese"— or "blue box," as it is known at Kraft—is a favorite with children and college students.

Tuna Salad Pie

Hot tuna salad in a biscuit crust—what could be easier or more attractive?

1 10-oz. can refrigerated
  biscuits
1½ cups (6 ozs.) shredded
  sharp cheddar cheese
1 6½-oz. can tuna,
  drained, flaked
¾ cup thin celery slices

⅓ cup Kraft real
  mayonnaise
2 tablespoons finely
  chopped onion
2 tablespoons chopped
  parsley
¼ teaspoon dill weed

Line 9-inch pie plate with biscuits, pressing edges together to seal. Bake at 350°, 5 minutes. Combine 1 cup cheese and remaining ingredients; spoon into biscuit shell. Bake at 350°, 25 minutes. Top with remaining cheese; continue baking until melted. 6 servings

Cheddar Cheese Pie

An American adaptation of the French quiche, this ham and cheese pie is a unique entrée for Sunday brunch, lunch or supper.

2 cups (8 ozs.) shredded
Kraft sharp cheddar
cheese
2 tablespoons flour
1½ cups milk
4 eggs, beaten

¾ cup finely chopped
ham
¼ teaspoon salt
Dash of pepper
1 9-inch unbaked pastry
shell

Toss cheese with flour. Add milk, eggs, ham and seasonings; mix well. Pour into pastry shell. Bake at 350°, 1 hour or until set. 6 servings

Variations: Substitute chopped cooked shrimp, sliced mushrooms or onion rings for ham. Add 2 tablespoons chopped parsley to egg mixture.

Serve a fresh fruit salad with Honey Fruit Dressing and this cheese pie as a late-evening supper.

Cheddar Strata

A 1920's "classic," strata was a featured attraction in school cafeterias throughout the nation at that time and is currently experiencing a resurgence in popularity.

12 dry white bread slices,
crusts trimmed
2 cups (8 ozs.) shredded
Kraft sharp cheddar
cheese

2½ cups milk
4 eggs, beaten
½ teaspoon salt
Dash of pepper

Place six bread slices on bottom of 11¾ × 7½-inch baking dish. Cover with 1½ cups cheese, remaining bread and cheese. Combine milk, eggs and seasonings; pour over bread. Refrigerate 1 hour. Bake at 350°, 50 to 55 minutes. 6 servings

Variations: Substitute shredded process American cheese for cheddar cheese. Add ⅓ cup finely chopped onion and ½ teaspoon basil leaves.

Classic Cheese Rabbit

This Kraft "classic" is based on a British savoury, a specialty of "Ye Olde Cheshire Cheese," one of the oldest pubs in London.

2 cups (8 ozs.) shredded
　Cracker Barrel sharp
　cheddar cheese
½ cup beer or ale

2 tablespoons margarine
½ teaspoon paprika
¼ teaspoon dry mustard
1 egg, slightly beaten

Heat ingredients, except egg, over low heat; stir until smooth. Stir small amount of hot mixture into egg; return to hot mixture. Cook, stirring constantly, until thickened; do not boil. Serve over toast. 4 servings

Variations: Add crisply cooked crumbled bacon slices, or top servings with French fried onions.

Rabbit is an excellent luncheon or supper dish served with a fruit or vegetable salad.

Cheese Fondue Surprise

A delectable—and beautiful—puff that can be prepared in advance.

1¾ cups milk
3 cups soft bread cubes
2 cups (8 ozs.) shredded
　Kraft sharp cheddar
　cheese

1 teaspoon salt
½ teaspoon dry mustard
¼ teaspoon pepper
4 eggs, separated

Heat milk. Add bread cubes, cheese and seasonings; stir until cheese is melted. Remove from heat. Gradually add slightly beaten egg yolks; cool. Fold in stiffly beaten egg whites; pour into 2-quart casserole. Cover; chill overnight. Bake at 325°, 1 hour and 10 minutes. Serve immediately. 6 to 8 servings

To bake immediately, decrease baking time to 50 minutes. Serve with a fruit salad and asparagus—they provide perfect complements for the tangy cheddar flavor of the fondue.

Country Breakfast

A proper breakfast to suit a ranch hand's hearty appetite, but an excellent lunch or supper dish by urban standards.

4 cups chopped cooked potatoes
½ cup chopped green pepper
2 tablespoons chopped onion
⅓ cup margarine
Salt and pepper
4 eggs
1 cup (4 ozs.) shredded Kraft sharp cheddar cheese

In 10-inch skillet, cook potatoes, green pepper and onion in margarine until lightly browned. Season to taste. Break eggs over potato mixture. Cover; cook until eggs are done. Top with cheese. Cover; continue cooking until cheese is melted. 4 servings

For lunch or supper, accompany this with marinated tomatoes and cucumber, and dark rye bread.

Four-Egg Cheese Soufflé

A Kraft "classic" that rises to almost any occasion.

3 tablespoons margarine
3 tablespoons flour
¾ cup milk
Dash of salt
Dash of cayenne
½ lb. Deluxe Choice•Old English process American cheese, cubed
4 eggs, separated

Make a white sauce with margarine, flour, milk and seasonings. Add cheese; stir until melted. Remove from heat. Gradually add slightly beaten egg yolks; cool. Fold into stiffly beaten egg whites; pour into 2-quart soufflé dish or casserole. With tip of spoon, make a slight indentation or "track" around top of soufflé 1 inch from edge to form a top hat. Bake at 300°, 1 hour. Serve immediately. 4 to 6 servings

Basic Soufflé Techniques: Separate the eggs while cold, but for stability and maximum volume, let the whites come to room temperature before beating. The whites should then be stiffly beaten—but not dry—before folding in the cheese sauce. Last word—don't open the oven door during baking.

Crepes Florentine

Delicate spinach crepes with a rich cheese sauce.

¾ cup milk
⅔ cup flour
3 eggs, beaten
½ teaspoon salt
   * * *
¼ cup margarine
¼ cup flour
1½ cups milk
 1 cup (4 ozs.) shredded
   Kraft Swiss cheese

¼ lb. process American
   cheese, shredded
2 10-oz. pkgs. frozen
   chopped spinach,
   cooked,
   well-drained
1 4-oz. can mushrooms,
   drained

Combine milk, flour, eggs and salt; beat until smooth. Let stand 30 minutes. For each crepe, pour ¼ cup batter into hot lightly greased 8-inch skillet. Cook until lightly browned on both sides.

Make a white sauce with margarine, flour and milk. Add Swiss and American cheese; stir until melted. Combine spinach, mushrooms and 1 cup cheese sauce. Fill each crepe with ⅓ cup spinach mixture; roll up. Place in 11¾ × 7½-inch baking dish; top with remaining cheese sauce. Bake at 350°, 20 to 25 minutes. 4 servings

Gourmet French Omelet

Omelets are traditional fare throughout Europe.

2 4-oz. cans mushrooms,
   drained
3 tablespoons margarine
6 eggs, slightly beaten
⅓ cup milk
   Salt and pepper

1 cup (4 ozs.) shredded
   Kraft sharp cheddar
   cheese
1 teaspoon finely
   chopped chives

Sauté mushrooms in 1 tablespoon margarine. Melt remaining margarine in 10-inch skillet over low heat. Combine eggs, milk and seasonings; pour into skillet. Cook slowly. As egg mixture sets, lift slightly with a spatula to allow uncooked portion to flow underneath. When set, place ¾ cup cheese, mushrooms and chives on half of omelet. Slip turner underneath, tip skillet to loosen and gently fold in half. Sprinkle with remaining cheese. 3 to 4 servings

Rinktum Ditty

Rinktum Ditty and Blushing Bunny are two crazy names for this delicious cheese rabbit, a favorite luncheon dish in the 1930s.

2 cups (8 ozs.) shredded
  Kraft sharp cheddar
  cheese
1 10¾-oz. can condensed
  tomato soup
2 tablespoons catsup

1 tablespoon finely
  chopped onion
½ teaspoon
  Worcestershire sauce
¼ teaspoon dry mustard
1 egg, slightly beaten

Heat ingredients, except egg, in saucepan over medium heat; stir until smooth. Stir small amount of hot mixture into egg; return to hot mixture. Cook, stirring constantly, until thickened; do not boil. Serve over toast. 4 servings

This rich cheddar sauce with a mild tomato flavor can be served over white, rye or whole-wheat toast, or crusty slices of warm French bread.

"Philly" Brunch Quiche

A complete meal in a crust, and a beautiful blend of flavors —cream cheese and ham, seasoned with dill.

1 8-oz. pkg. Philadelphia
  Brand cream cheese,
  cubed
1 cup milk
¼ cup chopped onion
1 tablespoon margarine
4 eggs, beaten

1 cup finely chopped
  ham
¼ cup chopped pimiento
¼ teaspoon dill weed
Dash of pepper
1 10-inch unbaked pastry
  shell

Heat cream cheese and milk over low heat; stir until smooth. Sauté onion in margarine. Gradually add cream cheese sauce to eggs; stir in onion, ham, pimiento and seasonings. Pour into pastry shell; bake at 350°, 35 to 40 minutes or until set. 8 servings

Take care not to overbake. The center will still be slightly soft when the quiche is done.

Ham 'n Swiss Frittata

A frittata is an Italian omelet served in a skillet, cut into wedges. Almost any meat, vegetable or cheese is at home here.

2 tablespoons margarine	¼ cup milk
6 eggs, slightly beaten	½ teaspoon salt
1 cup chopped ham	Dash of pepper
⅓ cup green onion slices	1 cup (4 ozs.) shredded
⅓ cup mayonnaise	Kraft Swiss cheese

Melt margarine in 10-inch oven-proof skillet or omelet pan over low heat. Combine ingredients except cheese; pour into skillet. Bake at 350°, 15 to 20 minutes. Top with cheese; continue baking until melted. 4 servings

Variations: Try frittata with bacon, sausage, pepperoni, salami—tomatoes, zucchini and beans—and mozzarella, parmesan or monterey jack cheese—or any other variations you can dream up!

Parmesan Soufflé

This crusty soufflé owes its piquant flavor to parmesan cheese. Serve as a main dish for brunch or lunch, a side dish at dinner.

¾ cup (3 ozs.) Kraft grated parmesan cheese	4 eggs, separated
3 tablespoons margarine	2 tablespoons chopped parsley
3 tablespoons flour	1 teaspoon prepared mustard
¾ cup milk	Dash of cayenne
¼ teaspoon salt	

Grease 1½-quart soufflé dish or casserole; coat with 2 tablespoons cheese. Make a white sauce with margarine, flour, milk and salt. Remove from heat. Gradually add slightly beaten egg yolks; cool. Stir in ½ cup cheese, parsley, mustard and cayenne. Fold into stiffly beaten egg whites. Pour into soufflé dish; sprinkle with remaining cheese. Bake at 375°, 30 to 35 minutes. Serve immediately. 6 servings

Hot rolls and a tossed salad are ideal accompaniments.

Top Hat Cheese Soufflé

The jaunty top-hat effect was originated by Mary Dahnke, the first director of the Kraft Kitchens. A home economist, she was employed in 1924 as the consumer's professional representative at Kraft.

⅓ cup margarine
⅓ cup flour
1½ cups milk
1 teaspoon salt
Dash of cayenne

2 cups (8 ozs.) shredded
  Cracker Barrel sharp
  cheddar cheese
6 eggs, separated

Make a white sauce with margarine, flour, milk and seasonings. Add cheese; stir until melted. Remove from heat. Gradually add slightly beaten egg yolks; cool. Fold into stiffly beaten egg whites; pour into 2-quart soufflé dish or casserole. With tip of spoon, make a slight indentation or "track" around top of soufflé 1 inch in from edge to form a top hat. Bake at 300°, 1 hour and 15 minutes. Serve immediately. 6 servings

Old-Fashioned Macaroni and Cheese

A family favorite and definitely a Kraft "classic"—this recipe first appeared in Kraft advertisements in the 1920s.

¼ cup margarine
¼ cup flour
2 cups milk
1 teaspoon salt
2 cups (8 ozs.) shredded
  Kraft sharp cheddar
  cheese

2 cups (7 ozs.) elbow
  macaroni, cooked,
  drained

Make a white sauce with margarine, flour, milk and salt. Add 1½ cups cheese; stir until melted. In 1½-quart casserole, layer half of macaroni and cheese sauce; repeat layers. Top with remaining cheese. Bake at 350°, 25 minutes. 6 to 8 servings

Santa Fe Brunch

This unique Southwestern concoction almost defies description—a scrambled combination of crisp fried tortillas, eggs, and monterey jack, highly seasoned with hot chilies and topped with spicy tomato sauce.

12 corn tortillas	1 teaspoon salt
⅓ cup oil	1 8-oz. pkg. Casino
1 cup chopped onion	monterey jack cheese,
10 eggs, beaten	cubed
1 tablespoon chopped	Chili Sauce
hot chili peppers	

Cut each tortilla into twelve wedges. Fry tortillas in hot oil until crisp, stirring frequently. Add onion; cook over medium heat 1 minute. Combine eggs, chili peppers and salt; pour over tortilla mixture. Stir gently until eggs begin to cook. Add cheese; mix lightly. Continue cooking until cheese is melted and eggs are done. Serve with:

Chili Sauce

1 8-oz. can tomato sauce	¼ teaspoon oregano
1 teaspoon chopped hot	leaves
chili peppers	¼ teaspoon garlic salt

Combine ingredients; simmer 15 minutes, stirring occasionally. 8 servings

Swiss Custard

A delicious custard to serve as a brunch or luncheon entrée.

1½ cups (6 ozs.) shredded	½ teaspoon salt
Kraft Swiss cheese	Dash of cayenne
4 eggs, beaten	Nutmeg
1½ cups milk	

Sprinkle cheese into six 6-oz. custard cups. Combine eggs, milk, salt and cayenne; pour over cheese. Sprinkle with nutmeg. Set custard cups in baking pan; pour in boiling water to ½-inch depth. Bake at 350°, 35 minutes. 6 servings

Savory Scrambled Eggs

Cream cheese keeps the eggs moist and creamy—an excellent recipe for brunch buffets, since the eggs hold well in a chafing dish.

2 tablespoons margarine
6 eggs, beaten
⅓ cup milk
   Salt and pepper

1 3-oz. pkg. Philadelphia
   Brand cream cheese,
   cubed

Melt margarine in skillet over low heat. Combine eggs, milk and seasonings; pour into skillet. Cook slowly until eggs begin to set. Add cream cheese; continue cooking, stirring occasionally, until cream cheese is melted and eggs are done. 4 servings

Variations: Add chopped parsley, chives, green onion slices or crisply cooked bacon, crumbled, as the eggs begin to set.

Golden Rice Casserole

A colorful cheese entrée for a meatless meal—Velveeta process cheese spread provides the necessary protein.

3 cups cooked rice
1 16-oz. can tomatoes,
   drained
1 4-oz. can mushrooms,
   drained
2 tablespoons chopped
   green pepper

2 tablespoons chopped
   onion
½ teaspoon salt
   Dash of pepper
½ lb. Velveeta process
   cheese spread, sliced

Combine ingredients except cheese spread; mix lightly. In 1½-quart casserole, layer half of rice mixture and cheese spread; repeat layers. Bake at 350°, 30 minutes. 4 servings

Variations: Substitute ½ cup chopped celery or ¼ cup ripe olive slices for mushrooms.

Complete the menu with a crisp lettuce salad and Easy Upside-Down Cake

Spaghetti Pie

Quick and easy—and everybody loves it.

1 pkg. Kraft Italian
  spaghetti dinner
2 eggs, beaten

1 6-oz. pkg. mozzarella
  cheese slices, cut into
  strips

Prepare spaghetti and sauce as directed on package. Add eggs and the grated parmesan cheese to spaghetti. In greased 9-inch pie plate, layer half of spaghetti mixture and mozzarella cheese; repeat layers. Bake at 350°, 10 minutes. Let stand 10 minutes before serving. Cut into wedges; serve with sauce. 6 servings

Kraft Italian spaghetti dinner was developed from an authentic Italian recipe. When Kraft introduced it in 1957, surveys revealed that many Italians had abandoned their traditional long-cooking sauces in favor of this convenience dinner.

Spinach Quiche

A complete meal in a pie—delicious and nutritious. If you like, substitute Swiss cheese for cheddar.

2 cups (8 ozs.) shredded
  Kraft sharp cheddar
  cheese
2 tablespoons flour
1 10-oz. pkg. frozen
  chopped spinach,
  cooked, well-drained
1 cup milk

2 eggs, beaten
3 crisply cooked bacon
  slices, crumbled
½ teaspoon salt
  Dash of pepper
1 9-inch unbaked pastry
  shell

Toss cheese with flour. Add spinach, milk, eggs, bacon and seasonings; mix well. Pour into pastry shell. Bake at 350°, 1 hour or until set. 6 servings

The secret of success is to shred the cheese very fine, and to drain the spinach *very* well. To ease last-minute preparation, prepare the bacon and the pastry shell in advance.

Saturday Supper

Macaroni and cheese with zucchini, an herb flavoring, and a crunchy cereal topping—deliciously different.

1 7¼-oz. pkg. Kraft macaroni and cheese dinner
1½ cups quartered zucchini slices
2 tablespoons margarine
1½ cups cottage cheese
½ teaspoon oregano leaves, crushed
½ teaspoon salt
Bite-size crispy rice squares

Prepare dinner as directed on package. Cook zucchini in margarine until tender. Add to dinner with cottage cheese and seasonings; mix lightly. Spoon into 1½-quart casserole; top with cereal. Bake at 375°, 35 minutes. 4 servings

Kraft macaroni and cheese dinner, a convenience dinner that dates back to the 1930s, is a quick and easy beginning for many casseroles and main dishes—an ideal way to use up leftover meats and vegetables deliciously.

Sunny Breakfast Eggs

Something different but easy for breakfast—scrambled eggs on English muffins, topped with smooth melting American Singles process cheese food.

3 tablespoons margarine
8 eggs
½ cup milk
2 tablespoons chopped pimiento
2 tablespoons chopped parsley
½ teaspoon salt
⅛ teaspoon pepper
4 English muffins, split, toasted
8 Kraft American Singles process cheese food, cut in half diagonally

Melt margarine in large skillet over low heat. Combine eggs, milk, pimiento, parsley and seasonings; pour into skillet. Cook slowly, stirring occasionally, until eggs are done. Spoon eggs onto muffins. Top with cheese food; broil until melted. 8 servings

The Kraft Story

1946–1950

May 7, 1947, marked Kraft's entry into television. "Kraft Television Theater" was an hour long, live drama viewed via 32,000 sets in Philadelphia and New York. Five years later, the estimated audience numbered twelve million.

Although television was in its infancy, Kraft recognized the great opportunity of providing both quality entertainment and visual product information. No actors appeared in the commercials, just pairs of hands that executed step-by-step food preparation. Before long the "hands" were renowned for demonstrating imaginative and practical food ideas. The voice of Ed Herlihy, the announcer who is still the narrator for many Kraft commercials, became synonymous with the motto "Kraft—for good food and good food ideas."

From the beginning the Kraft Kitchens were responsible for the recipes, approximately 360 per year, and preparation techniques. The recipes were developed by the staff in Chicago and sent, along with step-by-step photographs, to the 3-K studio at NBC in New York. There, hand models following the photographic instructions demonstrated the food ideas on "live" television. Today, the commercials are filmed, but the meticulous planning and original style remain unchanged. The service type commercials have helped establish Kraft as a trusted friend in homes across America.

After the war, research was resumed on a project that had concerned the cheese industry for years—cheese slices that could be pre-packaged for the retailer. In 1947, process cheese slices were test marketed. Once consumers were convinced that this was a quality cheese product, the sales volume was phenomenal. Today sliced cheese in many varieties is one of the most popular cheese items.

Another first during this period was the introduction of colored Parkay margarine. By 1948, several states had revised their food laws to permit the sale of yellow margarine. This was the first of many margarine innovations. Now margarine is available in many forms—sticks, tubs, soft, whipped, and liquid.

Sandwiches

Three centuries ago, the Earl of Sandwich started a trend that has become an American institution. An incurable gambler, it was his unusual habit to "sandwich" his meat between thick slices of bread when hunger overtook him at the gaming tables. Since those days the sandwich, named in the Earl's honor, has evolved!

Today, almost any food is at home in a sandwich. Variety and versatility are the valued qualities that have made the simple, or not so simple, sandwich a staple in the daily diet. Quick to make, easy to eat, and very satisfying, the sandwich is favorite fare for the lunch-bunch, brown-baggers, between-meal-snackers, and midnight-munchers.

Sandwiches are as satisfying to make as to eat—a great way to stretch your imagination. Start with an interesting bread or roll—coarse wheat, light or dark rye, Vienna, oatmeal, potato. Add a flavorful fruit, vegetable, or meat filling and a slice or two of cheese—cheddar, Swiss, mozzarella, muenster, provolone, American. Include a crispy leaf of lettuce. For a touch of class, serve your favorite combination open-style with a creamy sauce or dressing.

The recipes presented here are Kraft Kitchens' creations that have starred in television commercials and magazine ads. Whatever you wish—from a simple grilled cheese sandwich to an elegant frosted loaf—there are sandwiches to suit every situation.

Frosted Sandwich Loaf

A Kraft original and a "classic" from the elegant 1920s— do-ahead convenient, this loaf is still a favorite for showers and luncheons.

6 hard-cooked eggs, finely chopped
1 teaspoon prepared mustard
¼ teaspoon salt
Dash of pepper
Mayonnaise

* * *

2 cups finely chopped ham
¼ cup finely chopped sweet pickle
Mayonnaise

* * *

3 8-oz. pkgs. Philadelphia Brand cream cheese
¼ cup finely chopped watercress
Dash of salt and pepper

* * *

1 unsliced sandwich loaf, 16 inches long
Soft margarine
¼ cup milk

Combine eggs, mustard, seasonings and enough mayonnaise to moisten; mix lightly.

Combine meat, pickle and enough mayonnaise to moisten; mix lightly.

Combine ½ package softened cream cheese, watercress and seasonings, mixing until well blended.

Trim crust from bread; cut into four lengthwise slices. Spread bread slices with margarine. Spread one bread slice with egg salad, a second slice with ham salad, and a third slice with cream cheese mixture. Stack layers; cover with fourth bread slice. Combine remaining cream cheese and milk, mixing until well blended. Frost sandwich loaf; chill thoroughly.

Variations: Thinly sliced tomatoes or cucumbers or cheese slices may be substituted for either of the salad fillings.

Decorate the loaf with colorful garnishes such as sliced ripe or stuffed olives, radish roses, carrot curls or watercress.

Kraft was the first company to sponsor a full-hour, weekly television program.

Curried Egg Sandwiches

Curry and chopped ripe olives add far-eastern flavor to this basic egg salad—also try it as a filling for stuffed tomatoes.

4 hard-cooked eggs, chopped
¼ cup chopped pitted ripe olives
2 tablespoons chopped green pepper
½ teaspoon curry powder
Miracle Whip salad dressing
Salt and pepper
8 whole-wheat bread slices
Lettuce

Combine eggs, olives, green pepper, curry powder and enough salad dressing to moisten; mix lightly. Season to taste. For each sandwich, spread two bread slices with salad dressing; fill with egg salad and lettuce. Cut in half. 4 sandwiches

Variation: Add tomato slices; serve in toasted sesame buns or potato rolls.

Double-Decker Sandwiches

Hearty enough for a complete meal, special enough for entertaining.

2 cups finely chopped ham
⅓ cup chopped sweet pickle
1 tablespoon finely chopped onion
Kraft real mayonnaise
* * *
6 hard-cooked eggs, chopped
½ cup chopped celery
2 tablespoons chopped pimiento
Dash of salt
Kraft real mayonnaise
* * *
24 rye bread slices

Combine meat, pickle, onion and enough mayonnaise to moisten; mix lightly.

Combine eggs, celery, pimiento, salt and enough mayonnaise to moisten; mix lightly.

For each sandwich, spread one bread slice with ham salad. Cover with second bread slice spread with egg salad and third bread slice. Cut diagonally in half. 8 sandwiches

Serve with a fresh fruit salad and Swiss Chocolate Squares.

All-American Hero

Hero, hoagie, poor boy, gangplank, submarine—whatever you call it, this sandwich is an American tradition and a family favorite.

French bread loaf, cut in
  half lengthwise
Soft margarine
Lettuce
Tomato slices
Boiled ham slices
Kraft American Singles
  process cheese food
Coleslaw

Spread bread loaf with margarine; fill with lettuce, tomato, meat, cheese food and coleslaw.

A versatile sandwich, a hero can accommodate a variety of meats, vegetables and condiments. The creamy coleslaw in this version keeps the sandwich moist and fresh.

Open-Face Reubens

Open-style corned beef on rye toast, with Swiss cheese, onion rings, sauerkraut and a topping of tangy dressing—hearty and handsome!

Rye bread slices, toasted
Sauerkraut
Corned beef slices
Swiss cheese slices
Onion rings
Kraft thousand island
  dressing

Cover toast with sauerkraut, meat, cheese and onions. Serve open-style with dressing.

Crazy New Sandwich

Sounds good, tastes even better—and children are crazy about it!

White, raisin or
  whole-wheat bread
  slices
Kraft marshmallow creme
Creamy or chunk style
  peanut butter

For each sandwich, spread one bread slice with marshmallow creme; top with second bread slice spread with peanut butter. Cut diagonally in half.

114

Tuna Swiss Club

Triple-decker on toast pairs tuna salad with cucumber and Swiss cheese.

1 6½-oz. can tuna, drained, flaked
¼ cup chopped stuffed green olives
1 tablespoon chopped onion
Kraft real mayonnaise
12 white bread slices, toasted
Cucumber slices
Swiss cheese slices, cut in half

Combine tuna, olives, onion and enough mayonnaise to moisten; mix lightly. For each sandwich, spread three toast slices with mayonnaise. Cover one slice of toast with tuna salad and second slice of toast. Top with cucumber, cheese and third slice of toast. Cut into triangles. 4 sandwiches

If you're counting calories, omit two slices of bread and feel virtuous as you eat this salad sandwich open-style.

Special Club Sandwich

Two types of cheese make this a club with a difference.

White bread slices, toasted
Mayonnaise or salad dressing
Kraft sharp cheddar cheese slices, cut in half
Cooked chicken slices
Lettuce
Brick cheese slices, cut in half
Tomato slices
Crisply cooked bacon slices

For each sandwich, spread three toast slices with mayonnaise. Cover one toast slice with cheddar cheese, chicken, lettuce and second slice of toast. Top with brick cheese, tomato, bacon and third slice of toast. Cut into triangles; secure with picks.

To serve club-style, place the triangular sandwiches upright on a luncheon plate with potato chips and garnish with olives, pickles or radishes. Almost any cheese—Swiss, muenster or monterey jack—can substitute for cheddar.

Champion Sandwich

Egg salad, ham and Swiss—a winning combination.

6 hard-cooked eggs,
  chopped
¼ cup chopped celery
¼ cup chopped stuffed
  green olives
Salad dressing or
  mayonnaise

Salt and pepper
16 rye bread slices
8 boiled or baked ham
  slices
Kraft Swiss cheese
  slices, cut in half
Lettuce

Combine eggs, celery, olives and enough salad dressing to moisten; mix lightly. Season to taste. For each sandwich, spread two bread slices with salad dressing; fill with egg salad, meat, cheese and lettuce. Cut diagonally in half. 8 sandwiches

America's Favorite Sandwich

This open-style version of the famous "BLT" features Singles process cheese food.

White bread slices
Mayonnaise or salad
  dressing
Tomato slices

Kraft American Singles
  process cheese food
Crisply cooked bacon
  slices

For each sandwich, toast bread slice on one side; spread untoasted side with mayonnaise. Top with tomato, cheese food and bacon; broil until cheese food is melted.

Apple Dandy

A sandwich for breakfast? Why not, when it's this broiled cheese and apple treat.

White bread slices,
  toasted
Margarine
Velveeta process cheese
  spread, sliced

Thin apple slices
Brown sugar
Crisply cooked bacon slices

Spread toast with margarine. For each sandwich, cover toast slice with cheese spread and apple slices. Sprinkle lightly with brown sugar; broil until cheese spread is melted. Top with bacon.

Balboa Party Burgers

A Kraft "classic" and a very fancy burger—this is a Kraft Kitchens' favorite frequently served in the guest dining room.

½ cup Kraft real
   mayonnaise
½ cup dairy sour cream
½ cup finely chopped
   onion
2 tablespoons chopped
   parsley

* * *

2 lbs. ground beef

Salt and pepper
1 cup (4 ozs.) shredded
   Kraft sharp cheddar
   cheese
6 rye bread slices, toasted
   Soft margarine
   Lettuce
2 large tomatoes, sliced

Combine mayonnaise, sour cream, onion and parsley; mix well.

Shape meat into six oval patties. Broil on both sides to desired doneness. Season with salt and pepper. Top patties with sauce and cheese; broil until cheese is melted. Spread toast with margarine; top with lettuce, tomato and patties. 6 servings.

This hearty burger is almost a complete meal. For accompaniment, serve a tossed green salad and Apple Crisp.

Bun-Witch

Perfect for outdoor or fireplace cooking—the wrapped sandwiches can be heated directly on the grill or coals.

Hamburger buns, split
Soft margarine
Ham slices
Tomato slices
Thin onion slices

Kraft Swiss or muenster
   Singles process cheese
   food
Dill pickle slices

Spread buns with margarine; fill with meat, tomato, onion, cheese food and pickles. Wrap each sandwich in aluminum foil. Bake at 350°, 10 to 12 minutes or until heated.

Variation: For large quantities, place sandwiches on a 15½ × 10½-inch jelly roll pan. Cover securely with aluminum foil; bake at 350°, 20 minutes.

Barbecued Frank-Burgers

A teen favorite—franks and dill pickle in a "Sloppy Joe." Easy to make when you use tangy barbecue sauce.

½ lb. ground beef
½ lb. frankfurters, sliced
¾ cup Kraft barbecue
   sauce
⅓ cup chopped dill pickle

¼ cup chopped onion
6 hamburger buns
   American process
   cheese food

Brown beef; drain. Stir in frankfurters, barbecue sauce, pickle and onion. Cover; simmer 15 minutes. Fill buns with meat mixture and cheese food. 6 sandwiches

Occasionally substitute canned luncheon meat for franks and chopped green pepper or olives for dill pickle.

Franks 'n Crescents

Quick frank and cheddar wrap-ups made with convenient crescent roll dough.

8 frankfurters, partially
   split
Kraft sharp cheddar
   cheese, cut into strips

1 8-oz. can refrigerated
   crescent rolls

Fill each frankfurter with cheese strip. Separate crescent dough into eight triangles. Place frankfurter on wide end of each triangle; roll up. Place on greased cookie sheet, cheese side up. Bake at 375°, 15 minutes or until rolls are golden brown. 8 servings

Cartwheel Franks

Franks curl as they broil, forming "wheels"—an intriguing idea for children, and a convenient way to serve frankfurters on round buns.

Frankfurters
Hamburger buns, split,
   toasted

Cheez Whiz process cheese
   spread

Cut frankfurters almost through at ½-inch intervals. Broil until frankfurters curl. Place on bottom halves of buns; fill centers with cheese spread. Serve with top halves of buns.

Grilled Reuben Sandwiches

The famous Reuben! It's impossible to improve on the original—but some ask for thousand island dressing or sour cream.

Rye bread slices
Kraft Swiss cheese slices,
  cut in half

Corned beef slices
Sauerkraut
Soft margarine

For each sandwich, fill two bread slices with cheese, meat and sauerkraut. Spread outside of sandwich with margarine; grill on both sides until lightly browned. Cut in half.

Boston Burgers

Old-fashioned favorite from the 1930s. Economical beans were a "stretcher" for the more expensive ground beef, which was sometimes omitted entirely.

½ lb. ground beef
¼ cup chopped onion
1 22-oz. can baked beans
¼ cup chili sauce
½ teaspoon salt
  Dash of pepper

8 hamburger buns, split,
  toasted
1 4-oz. pkg. Kraft
  shredded sharp
  cheddar cheese

Brown meat; drain. Add onion; cook until tender. Stir in beans, chili sauce and seasonings. Cover; simmer 20 minutes. Fill buns with meat mixture and cheese. 8 sandwiches

Cheese Long Loaf

Attractive, crusty accompaniment for soups and salads— bring it to the table in a napkin-lined basket or on a bread board.

French bread loaf
Margarine, melted
Tomato slices

Deluxe Choice process
  American cheese slices,
  cut in half diagonally

Cut loaf into slices to within ½ inch of bottom crust. Brush slices with margarine; place on ungreased cookie sheet. Bake at 400°, 10 minutes. Insert tomato and cheese between bread slices; continue baking until tomatoes are hot and cheese is melted.

Devonshire Muffins

A colorful open-style sandwich with two unique features—
caraway cheese and sandwich spread.

English muffins, split,
  toasted
Kraft sandwich spread
Tomato slices

Caraway cheese slices,
  cut in half
Crisply cooked bácon
  slices

Spread muffins with sandwich spread. Cover with tomato and cheese; broil until cheese is melted. Top with bacon.

Wonder Grills

The "wonder" of this grilled treat is Miracle Whip salad
dressing—the sandwich browns beautifully!

White bread slices
Prepared mustard
Luncheon meat
  slices

Velveeta process cheese
  spread, sliced
Miracle Whip salad
  dressing

For each sandwich, spread two bread slices with mustard; fill with meat and cheese spread. Spread outside of sandwich with salad dressing; grill over low heat until lightly browned on both sides.

Select the luncheon meat of your choice, and occasionally substitute cheddar, mozzarella or Swiss cheese for the Velveeta process cheese spread.

Quick Golden Grill

Velveeta process cheese spread was first introduced in 1928.
One of its original uses was this all-time favorite grilled
sandwich.

White bread slices
Velveeta process cheese
  spread, sliced

Soft margarine

For each sandwich, fill two bread slices with cheese spread. Spread outside of sandwich with margarine; grill until lightly browned on both sides. Cut in half.

Milano Burgers

Dressed-up burgers—Italian dressing and parmesan cheese lend unique flavor.

1 lb. ground beef	6 Vienna bread slices
Kraft Italian dressing	¼ cup (1 oz.) grated
⅓ cup dry bread crumbs	parmesan cheese
1 egg, beaten	6 tomato slices
2 tablespoons chopped	6 small green pepper
onion	rings

Combine meat, ⅓ cup dressing, crumbs, egg and onion; mix lightly. Shape into six oval patties. Broil on both sides to desired doneness. Brush one side of bread with dressing; sprinkle with cheese. Broil until lightly browned. Top with meat patties, tomato and green pepper. Sprinkle with additional cheese; broil 1 to 2 minutes. 6 servings

Variation: Omit parmesan cheese. Substitute Golden Caesar dressing from Kraft for Italian dressing.

Serve with coleslaw and fresh fruit to round out a delightful meal.

Jaunty Joes

Kraft's version of the "Sloppy Joe"—spicy barbecue sauce provides the special seasoning, melted cheese the finishing touch.

1 lb. ground beef	½ teaspoon salt
½ cup chopped green	1 cup Kraft barbecue
pepper	sauce
½ cup chopped celery	8 hamburger buns, split
½ cup chopped onion	1 8-oz. pkg. process
1 tablespoon flour	American cheese slices

Brown meat; drain. Add vegetables, flour and salt; mix well. Stir in barbecue sauce; simmer 15 minutes. Cover bottom halves of buns with meat sauce and cheese; broil until cheese is melted. Serve with top halves of buns. 8 sandwiches

Serve with a crisp green salad and Crunchies for dessert.

Stromboli Sandwich

Tasty Italian sandwich . . . great for the family or casual parties and a special favorite of teenagers.

1 lb. mild Italian sausage
½ lb. ground beef
1 cup chopped onion
½ cup chopped green pepper
1 4-oz. can mushrooms, drained
1 8-oz. can tomato sauce
1 6-oz. can tomato paste
¼ cup water
¼ cup (1 oz.) grated parmesan cheese
¼ teaspoon oregano leaves, crushed
¼ teaspoon garlic salt
¼ teaspoon rosemary, crushed
1 Vienna bread loaf
1 6-oz. pkg. Kraft mozzarella cheese slices, cut in half

Remove sausage from casing. Brown meat; drain. Add vegetables; cook 5 minutes. Stir in tomato sauce, tomato paste, water, parmesan cheese and seasonings. Simmer 10 minutes, stirring occasionally. Cut lengthwise slice from top of bread; scoop out center, leaving a 1-inch shell. Place half of mozzarella cheese in shell; fill with hot meat mixture. Cover with remaining cheese and top bread slice. Wrap in aluminum foil. Bake at 400°, 6 to 8 minutes. 8 servings

Texas Tacos

A typical taco with a special flavor feature—barbecue sauce.

1 lb. ground beef
2 tablespoons chopped onion
½ cup Kraft barbecue sauce
Salt and pepper
10 taco shells
2 cups shredded lettuce
1½ cups (6 ozs.) shredded cheddar or monterey jack cheese

Brown meat; drain. Add onion; cook until tender. Stir in barbecue sauce; simmer 5 minutes. Season to taste. Fill taco shells with lettuce, meat sauce and cheese. 10 tacos

Great for do-it-yourself buffet entertaining. Along with the taco basics, arrange bowls of extra toppings such as sour cream, guacamole, chopped tomatoes and chilies.

Swiss Fondue Sandwich

A hot sandwich was never so delicious as this one topped with a rich fondue sauce—an imaginative use for leftover turkey.

Margarine
3 tablespoons flour
½ teaspoon salt
Dash of pepper
1 cup milk
1 cup chicken broth or bouillon

1 8-oz. pkg. Kraft Swiss cheese slices, cut into strips
6 white bread slices, toasted
Sliced cooked turkey
Paprika

Melt 3 tablespoons margarine over low heat; blend in flour and seasonings. Gradually add milk and broth; cook, stirring constantly, until thickened. Add cheese; stir until melted. Spread toast with margarine; cover with turkey and sauce. Serve open-style; sprinkle with paprika. 6 sandwiches

Variation: For an extra touch of color and elegance, add broccoli or asparagus spears before topping with sauce. Sprinkle with toasted sesame seeds or sliced almonds.

Tuna Salad Burgers

Anyone who has ever lived in a dormitory must have encountered this hot tuna salad bunwich—also known as a "Friday Burger."

1 6½-oz. can tuna, drained, flaked
¼ lb. Deluxe Choice process American cheese, cubed
3 hard-cooked eggs, chopped

⅓ cup salad dressing or mayonnaise
¼ cup sweet pickle relish
Salt and pepper
6 hamburger buns, split

Combine tuna, cheese, eggs, salad dressing and relish; mix well. Season to taste. Fill buns with tuna salad; wrap each in aluminum foil. Place on cookie sheet. Bake at 375°, 15 to 20 minutes or until heated. 6 sandwiches

Easy do-ahead for a crowd—sandwiches can be completely prepared, wrapped and refrigerated, ready for reheating.

The Kraft Story

1951–1958

Kraft celebrated its Golden Anniversary in 1953—a half century of remarkable progress. Reminiscing to his employees, J. L. Kraft said, "I view each one of the past fifty years with affectionate remembrance and deep satisfaction. And if one thing stands out above all achievements, it is the deep abiding human values plowed into this business....
I see this milestone not so much as the ending of the fiftieth year but as the beginning of the fifty-first....Who can set a boundary to the achievements of any individual—or many individuals working together in common cause—over a single day, or decade or century?"

In 1903, the company's total assets were small but promising—a man with a vision, $65 capital, a small stock of cheese, and a faithful horse. As Kraft entered its fifty-first year, J. L. Kraft's "dream" had grown into one of the largest food companies in the world with operations in 43 states, 8 Canadian provinces, and 3 foreign countries. Its assets now numbered 15,000 employees, over 200 diversified food products, dozens of production plants, 1,400 salesmen, and a fleet of 1,200 delivery trucks. Quite an accomplishment for a farm boy from Ft. Erie! These had indeed been golden years for Kraft.

Fulfilling J. L.'s pledge, the company continued to diversify and extend its product lines. In 1952, Kraft introduced Cheez Whiz process cheese spread, a convenience sauce which could be used directly from the jar. Two years later, through the acquisition of a marshmallow plant, another innovative product was marketed— Kraft miniature marshmallows. These tiny marshmallows were specifically designed for ingredient use in fruit and gelatin salads and desserts.

In 1957, Miracle Brand margarine was introduced. It was the first whipped margarine in stick form and was immediately popular with consumers due to its easy spreading and blending qualities. Kraft barbecue sauce, developed from a Kraft Kitchens' recipe, was successfully marketed in 1958 at a time when outdoor barbecuing was not yet an American tradition. Other new Kraft products included a line of jellies and preserves, dessert toppings, refrigerated citrus fruit and juices, and cheese dips.

Salads

The word "salad" dates back to the days of Caesar when Romans sprinkled "sal" (salt) on their salads. Long before then, however, people were eating salad or salad-type foods. Primitive man sampled sweet grasses, pungent herbs, and savory weeds. The ancient Egyptians were skilled in the art of mixing oil, vinegar, and Oriental spices which they poured over greens. The Greeks served salads as a final course—a fresh crisp ending after sweets.

It was much later that salads gained prestige in the courts of the European monarchs. Royal salad makers combined as many as thirty-five ingredients in a giant serving bowl. Favored ingredients included parsley, parsnips, fennel, angelica, young primrose, violets, sage, and marjoram. In the elegant 1890s, wealthy American hostesses imported French chefs to mix their salads. Salads, however, were to remain somewhat of a novelty to most Americans until the late 1920s or early 1930s.

Almost any food is salad suitable—fresh, canned, or frozen fruits and vegetables; meat; fish; poultry; macaroni; rice; cheese. Variety in salad making is limited only by one's imagination. Consider the long list of basic salads—coleslaw, potato salad, macaroni salad, Waldorf salad, 24-hour salad, tossed salad, vegetable relishes, fruit salad, and ambrosia.

The Kraft Kitchens' file of favorite salads dates back to the 1930s. Some of the most requested recipes are presented here. Colorful, crisp, creamy, molded, simple, fancy, light, hearty—something for every occasion.

Spinach Salad

Delicious as an appetizer course or as an accompaniment with the entrée.

2 qts. (1 lb.) torn spinach
4 crisply cooked bacon
   slices, crumbled
   Onion rings

3 hard-cooked eggs,
   chopped
Kraft Italian or Golden
   caesar dressing

Combine spinach, bacon, onions, eggs and enough dressing to moisten; toss lightly. 6 to 8 servings

For a wilted salad, heat the dressing and toss with the greens just before serving.

Carrot Raisin Salad

A family favorite that's particularly popular with children.

1½ cups grated carrots
¾ cup chopped celery
½ cup raisins

Miracle Whip salad
   dressing

Combine carrots, celery, raisins and enough salad dressing to moisten; toss lightly. Chill. 4 servings

For variety add crushed pineapple, shredded cabbage, chopped apples or green grapes.

Harvest Coleslaw

Cheddar cheese and tomatoes are flavorful additions to basic coleslaw.

1 qt. shredded cabbage
½ cup chopped celery
¼ cup green onion slices
¼ cup radish slices

Miracle Whip salad
   dressing
1 cup chopped tomato
Sharp cheddar cheese,
   shredded

Combine cabbage, celery, onions, radishes and enough salad dressing to moisten; toss lightly. Chill. Add tomato just before serving; sprinkle with cheese. 6 to 8 servings

Variation: Omit chopped tomato; serve on tomato slices or in tomato cups.

Golden Potato Salad

Traditional midwestern potato salad—always welcome at reunions, picnics, cookouts, casual parties and everyday family meals.

4 cups chopped cooked
  potatoes
1 cup celery slices
4 hard-cooked eggs,
  chopped
1 tablespoon chopped
  pimiento

1 teaspoon salt
  Dash of pepper
½ cup Miracle Whip
  salad dressing
2 tablespoons prepared
  mustard

Combine potatoes, celery, eggs, pimiento and seasonings. Add combined salad dressing and mustard; mix lightly. Chill. Add additional salad dressing before serving, if desired. 6 to 8 servings

Cold potato salads are best when prepared a day in advance.

Kidney Bean Salad

A favorite summer salad. Keep a supply available in the refrigerator for quick snacks, light suppers or picnics.

1 16-oz. can kidney
  beans, drained
1 cup celery slices
½ cup chopped pickles
2 tablespoons chopped
  pimiento

2 tablespoons chopped
  green pepper
1 tablespoon finely
  chopped onion
  Dash of pepper
  Kraft real mayonnaise
  Lettuce

Combine vegetables, pepper and enough mayonnaise to moisten; mix lightly. Chill. Serve in lettuce-lined bowl. 4 to 6 servings

Variation: Substitute creamy cucumber dressing for mayonnaise. Garnish with hard-cooked egg slices and parsley sprigs.

Perry Como first appeared as host for the "Kraft Music Hall" in 1959. By that time, the program was televised by 200 stations throughout the United States and Canada.

Majestic Layered Salad

Do-ahead salad with a secret—mayonnaise seals in flavor and freshness.

1 qt. shredded lettuce
2 cups mushroom slices
1½ cups red onion rings
2 10-oz. pkgs. frozen
   peas, cooked,
   drained

1 cup Kraft real
   mayonnaise
½ teaspoon sugar
½ teaspoon curry powder
2 crisply cooked bacon
   slices, crumbled

In 2½-quart salad bowl, layer lettuce, mushrooms, onions and peas. Combine mayonnaise, sugar and curry powder. Spread over salad to seal. Cover; refrigerate overnight. Top with bacon before serving. 8 servings

Variations: Substitute dill weed for curry. For a main-dish salad, add a layer of chopped cooked chicken, turkey or ham.

Party Potato Salad

Shredded carrots, sour cream and a hint of dill transform a simple potato salad into a festive and flavorful dish.

6 cups chopped cooked
   potatoes
1 medium cucumber,
   sliced
1 cup shredded carrots
1 tablespoon chopped
   chives

2 teaspoons salt
½ teaspoon dill seed
   Dash of pepper
1 cup dairy sour cream
½ cup Miracle Whip
   salad dressing

Combine potatoes, cucumber, ¾ cup carrots, chives and seasonings. Add combined sour cream and salad dressing; mix lightly. Chill. Garnish with remaining carrots. 8 to 10 servings

In the early fifties the first photography studio was established in the Chicago office. The intent was to provide a staff of professional photographers who knew Kraft products, were experts in food photography, and could work cooperatively with the Kraft Kitchens. Today the department is a full scale creative services operation. In addition to a staff of photographers, it employs artists, writers, and audio-visual experts.

Three Bean Salad

A long-time American favorite that varies from region to region depending on what beans—red, pinto, garbanzo or wax—are indigenous to the area.

1 16-oz. can cut green
   beans, drained
1 16-oz. can lima beans,
   drained
1 16-oz. can kidney
   beans, drained

1 cup chopped tomato
1 cup celery slices
½ cup chopped sweet
   pickles
Kraft or Catalina
   French dressing

Combine vegetables and enough dressing to moisten; toss lightly. Chill. 10 to 12 servings

Vegetable Macedoine Platter

Entertain with ease by letting guests make their own salads.

Sliced tomatoes
Cooked peas
Radish slices
Carrot sticks
Cucumber slices

Green onion slices
Leaf lettuce
Kraft Italian, French or
   thousand island dressing

Arrange vegetables in groups on lettuce-covered platter. Serve with dressing.

For extra flavor, marinate some of the vegetables in Italian or French dressing.

Midsummer Macaroni Salad

If you've never made macaroni salad with macaroni and cheese dinner, this is a must.

1 7¼-oz. pkg. Kraft
   macaroni and
   cheese dinner
1 cup celery slices
1 cup chopped tomato
⅔ cup salad dressing or
   mayonnaise

½ cup chopped onion
½ cup chopped sweet
   pickles
2 tablespoons prepared
   mustard

Prepare dinner as directed on package. Add remaining ingredients; mix lightly. Chill. Add additional salad dressing before serving, if desired. 6 to 8 servings

Southwest Bean Salad

Perfect for casual entertaining and outdoor dining—a good do-ahead, since flavor improves as ingredients mingle with dressing. Double or triple the recipe, depending on the size of the crowd.

1 8-oz. bottle Kraft herb and garlic French dressing
1 16-oz. can pinto or kidney beans, drained
1 16-oz. can garbanzo beans, drained
1 cup celery slices
½ cup pitted ripe olive slices
½ cup radish slices
⅓ cup green onion slices
⅓ cup pimiento strips
Lettuce

Pour dressing over vegetables. Cover; marinate in refrigerator several hours or overnight. Serve in lettuce-lined bowl. 8 to 10 servings

Riviera Garden Salad

This Kraft "classic" appeared on the dinner label for many years and still retains its popularity.

1 7¼-oz. pkg. Kraft macaroni and cheese dinner
1 cup chopped tomato
1 cup chopped cucumber
½ cup dairy sour cream
¼ cup radish slices
¼ cup chopped green pepper
¼ cup salad dressing or mayonnaise
¼ teaspoon salt
Dash of pepper

Prepare dinner as directed on package. Add remaining ingredients; mix lightly. Chill. Add additional salad dressing before serving, if desired. 4 to 6 servings

In 1953, Kraft was the first company to present food commercials in color. By 1956, all of its commercials and shows were in color. This greatly enhanced the appearance of the food in the close-up photography.

Pompeian Salad

This Greek-style salad should be carefully arranged to show off colorful ingredients. Depending on size of serving, the salad can be offered as an appetizer, accompaniment or main-dish salad.

Tomato wedges	Casino blue cheese,
Hard-cooked egg wedges	crumbled
Pitted ripe olives	Oregano
Anchovy fillets	Italian dressing
Shredded lettuce	

For each salad, arrange tomato, eggs, olives and anchovies on lettuce. Top with cheese and oregano; serve with dressing.

Waldorf Party Salad

A special-occasion Waldorf made with grapes and a fluffy whipped cream dressing. Serve in a lettuce-lined bowl or in individual lettuce cups.

3 cups chopped apples	½ cup salad dressing or
1 cup grape halves	mayonnaise
1 cup Kraft miniature	½ cup heavy cream,
marshmallows	whipped
½ cup walnut halves	

Combine fruit, marshmallows, nuts and salad dressing; toss lightly. Fold in whipped cream. Chill. 4 to 6 servings

Toss the apples with a small amount of orange, lemon or pineapple juice to prevent discoloration if the salad is to be held several hours. Thoroughly drain the apples before combining with the other ingredients.

In 1957, Kraft expanded its dressing line in response to the growing interest in a wide variety of salads. Catalina Brand French dressing, Kraft oil and vinegar dressing, and Kraft thousand island dressing in a pourable form were introduced.

Grape Cluster Salad

A Kraft "classic" from the 1930s—these decorative grape-studded pears are especially attractive arranged on a platter lined with leaf or bibb lettuce.

1 3-oz. pkg. Philadelphia Brand cream cheese	8 pear halves
3 tablespoons salad dressing or mayonnaise	2 cups grape halves

Combine softened cream cheese and salad dressing, mixing until well blended. Thoroughly dry pear halves. Frost rounded sides with cream cheese mixture; cover with grapes. Chill. 8 servings

Pineapple Coleslaw

This colorful family favorite, a Kraft "classic," introduced fruit to slaw.

1 qt. shredded cabbage	1 cup chopped apple
1 cup miniature marshmallows	½ cup chopped celery
1 8¼-oz. can pineapple chunks, drained	Miracle Whip salad dressing

Combine cabbage, marshmallows, pineapple, apple, celery and enough salad dressing to moisten; toss lightly. Chill. 10 to 12 servings

Watermelon Marshmallow Boat

Almost any fresh fruit is at home in a melon boat, and variety makes a colorful salad. Select a melon to suit the size of the gathering.

Watermelon	Strawberries
Kraft miniature marshmallows	Grapes
Banana chunks	Blueberries
	Peach slices

Cut off top third of watermelon. Scoop out melon balls, leaving 2-inch shell. Cut edge of shell in zig-zag design. Combine melon balls, marshmallows and remaining fruit; toss lightly. Spoon fruit mixture into shell.

Heritage Fruit Salad

Colorful ambrosia with a fluffy coconut-honey dressing. An excellent accompaniment or dessert salad to serve buffet-style in a decorative glass bowl.

1 32-oz. jar Kraft fruit
    salad, drained
1 cup strawberry halves
1 cup melon balls

1 banana, sliced
Coconut Cream
    Dressing

Combine fruit; chill. Serve with:

Coconut Cream Dressing

⅓ cup salad dressing or
    mayonnaise
1 tablespoon honey

⅓ cup heavy cream,
    whipped
3 tablespoons flaked
    coconut

Combine salad dressing and honey; mix well. Fold in whipped cream and coconut. Chill. 6 servings

Sonora Fruit Salad

A do-ahead party salad—at its best when prepared a day in advance.

1 11-oz. can mandarin
    orange segments
½ cup Kraft real
    mayonnaise
½ cup dairy sour cream
2 bananas, sliced

1 8¼-oz. can pineapple
    chunks, drained
1 cup miniature
    marshmallows
½ cup shredded coconut

Drain orange segments, reserving 2 tablespoons syrup. Combine syrup, mayonnaise and sour cream; mix well. Add orange segments and remaining ingredients; mix lightly. Chill several hours or overnight. 8 servings

Vary the fruit as you wish, but be sure to select those that will keep well overnight, such as apricots, peaches or cherries. Berries should be added just before serving. Like all salads, this creamy fruit mixture should be kept tightly covered in the refrigerator.

Tomato Royal

This attractive luncheon favorite is a Kraft "classic."

6 hard-cooked eggs,
  chopped
3 tablespoons chopped
  green pepper
½ teaspoon curry powder

¼ teaspoon salt
  Miracle Whip salad
  dressing
4 tomatoes

Combine eggs, green pepper, seasonings and enough salad dressing to moisten; mix lightly. Cut each tomato into six sections, almost to stem end; fill with egg salad. 4 servings

Shrimp 'n Rice Salad

A glamorous seafood salad for entertaining.

3 cups cooked rice
1 lb. frozen cleaned
  shrimp, cooked
1 10-oz. pkg. frozen peas,
  cooked, drained

1 cup Kraft real
  mayonnaise
¾ cup celery slices
2 tablespoons chopped
  onion
Salt and pepper

Combine ingredients except salt and pepper; mix lightly. Season to taste. Chill. 4 to 6 servings

Serve this main-dish salad in a clear glass bowl or mounded on a bed of crisp lettuce. Garnish with cucumber and tomato slices.

Chicken Salad Superb

Delicious for summer dining! This special chicken salad can be served in pineapple halves, honeydew melon wedges or lettuce cups.

2½ cups chopped cooked
  chicken
1 cup chopped celery

1 cup chopped apple
1 cup grape halves
  Kraft real mayonnaise

Combine chicken, celery, fruit and enough mayonnaise to moisten; toss lightly. Chill. 6 servings

Variation: Pineapple chunks, nectarine slices or melon balls can be substituted for the apples.

Calcutta Turkey Salad

An epicurean salad for entertaining (and an excellent use of leftover turkey)—Roka blue cheese dressing and curry are a unique flavor combination that complements the other ingredients.

2 cups chopped cooked
    turkey
1 11-oz. can mandarin
    orange segments,
    drained
½ cup chopped green
    pepper

½ cup celery slices
½ cup Roka blue cheese
    dressing
½ teaspoon curry powder
Lettuce

Combine turkey, oranges, green pepper and celery. Add combined dressing and curry powder; toss lightly. Serve in lettuce-lined bowl. 6 to 8 servings

With colorful accompaniments, such as coconut, walnuts, chopped hard-cooked eggs and crisply cooked bacon, this is a dramatic salad. Arrange it buffet-style and let guests help themselves. To complete the menu, add Rye Lace and Tahiti Cream Pie.

Dilly Tuna Salad

A dieter's delight, this refreshing salad combines several low-calorie foods with flavorful low-calorie dressings.

1½ cups cottage cheese
1 6½-oz. can tuna,
    drained, flaked
⅓ cup Kraft low calorie
    thousand island or
    French dressing
¼ cup chopped celery

¼ cup chopped green
    pepper
¼ cup chopped onion
¼ teaspoon dill weed
Salt and pepper
Lettuce

Combine cottage cheese, tuna, dressing, celery, green pepper, onion and dill weed; mix lightly. Season to taste. Chill. Serve on lettuce. 4 servings

For variety, add shredded carrot or chopped cucumber, and serve with sliced tomatoes or in tomato cups.

Super Strata Salad

A layered-look party salad that's absolutely gorgeous. Arrange the colorful ingredients in a large shallow bowl or on dinner plates.

2 qts. shredded lettuce
12 tomato slices
12 peeled avocado slices
3 hard-cooked eggs, sliced
2 cups cooked turkey or chicken strips
¼ cup red onion rings
2 crisply cooked bacon slices, crumbled
Watercress
Kraft thousand island dressing

Layer lettuce, tomatoes, avocados, eggs, turkey and onions in salad bowl; sprinkle with bacon. Chill. Garnish with watercress. Serve with dressing. 6 servings

To vary the salad, add a layer of shredded cheddar or Swiss cheese and substitute croutons for bacon. Almost any dressing is compatible with this salad—try creamy cucumber, French or caesar.

Salmon Supper Salad

A complete meal in a salad, made with a convenience dinner —another time, substitute chopped cooked chicken for the salmon.

1 7¼-oz. pkg. Kraft macaroni and cheese dinner
1 7¾-oz. can salmon, drained, flaked
¾ cup salad dressing or mayonnaise
½ cup chopped cucumber
¼ cup radish slices
2 tablespoons finely chopped onion
Dash of salt and pepper

Prepare dinner as directed on package. Add remaining ingredients; mix lightly. Chill. Add additional salad dressing before serving, if desired. 4 to 6 servings

As in all pasta, rice or potato salads, the macaroni absorbs moisture as it chills, so you may want to add extra salad dressing before serving.

Mexican Salad

Simply spectacular! Hot salad made with meat sauce, shredded lettuce, sharp cheddar—festive and different for entertaining or family suppers.

1 lb. ground beef
¼ cup chopped onion
1 16-oz. can kidney
    beans, drained
½ cup Catalina French
    dressing
½ cup water

1 tablespoon chili
    powder
1 qt. shredded lettuce
½ cup green onion slices
2 cups (8 ozs.) shredded
    Kraft sharp cheddar
    cheese

Brown meat; drain. Add onion; cook until tender. Stir in beans, dressing, water and chili powder; simmer 15 minutes. Combine lettuce and green onion. Add meat mixture and 1½ cups cheese; mix lightly. Top with remaining cheese. 4 to 6 servings

For variety, serve with toppings such as sour cream, sliced avocado, tortilla chips and sliced ripe olives.

Salade Niçoise

A Kraft variation of a traditional French salad—a delicious way to use leftovers, because almost any meat or vegetable can be added.

4 cups cooked potato
    slices
1 9-oz. pkg. frozen cut
    green beans, cooked,
    drained
½ cup chopped onion
    Kraft Italian dressing
    Lettuce
3 tomatoes, cut into
    wedges

3 hard-cooked eggs, cut
    into wedges
    Anchovy fillets
    Pitted ripe olives
1 6½-oz. can tuna,
    drained, flaked
    Capers

Combine potatoes, beans, onion and ½ cup dressing; toss lightly. Cover; chill several hours or overnight. Add additional dressing to potato mixture to moisten; mix lightly. Place in center of lettuce-lined platter; surround with tomatoes, eggs, anchovies, olives and tuna. Sprinkle with capers; serve with additional dressing. 6 servings

142

Cranberry Crimson Mold

Made with convenience products, this pretty, flavorful mold requires very little preparation.

2 3-oz. pkgs. strawberry
flavored gelatin
1½ cups boiling water
1 cup Miracle Whip
salad dressing

1 10-oz. pkg. frozen
cranberry-orange
relish, thawed
1½ cups applesauce

Dissolve gelatin in boiling water; cool. Gradually add to salad dressing, mixing until blended. Chill until partially set; fold in relish and applesauce. Pour into 6-cup ring mold; chill until firm. Unmold. 6 to 8 servings

Creamy Orange Salad

Surround with fresh strawberries, blueberries, green grapes or peach slices.

1 3-oz. pkg. orange
flavored gelatin
1½ cups boiling water
1 8-oz. pkg. Philadelphia
Brand cream cheese

¼ cup orange juice
1 tablespoon lemon juice
1 tablespoon grated
orange rind
Lettuce

Dissolve gelatin in boiling water. Gradually add to softened cream cheese, mixing until well blended. Stir in juices and rind. Pour into 1-quart mold; chill until firm. Unmold; surround with lettuce. 4 to 6 servings

Frosty Cucumber Mold

An ideal companion for ham, chicken or salmon.

1 3-oz. pkg. lime flavored
gelatin
½ teaspoon salt
1 cup boiling water
1 cup Kraft real
mayonnaise

½ cup dairy sour cream
1 cup chopped peeled
cucumber
¼ cup chopped pimiento
1 tablespoon finely
chopped onion

Dissolve gelatin and salt in boiling water; cool. Combine mayonnaise and sour cream; mix well. Gradually add gelatin mixture to mayonnaise mixture. Chill until partially set; fold in cucumber, pimiento and onion. Pour into 1-quart mold; chill until firm. Unmold. 4 to 6 servings

Green Garden Salad

An adaptation of Perfection Salad—popular in the 1940s.

1 3-oz. pkg. lemon
    flavored gelatin
½ teaspoon salt
1 cup boiling water
1 cup milk
2 tablespoons vinegar
½ cup Kraft real
    mayonnaise

½ cup chopped celery
½ cup shredded cabbage
½ cup shredded carrots
2 tablespoons chopped
    green pepper
1 tablespoon finely
    chopped onion

Dissolve gelatin and salt in boiling water; cool. Gradually add gelatin mixture, milk and vinegar to mayonnaise, mixing until blended. Chill until partially set; fold in vegetables. Pour into 1-quart mold or six ¾-cup molds; chill until firm. Unmold. 6 servings

Guacamole Ring

Particularly suited to Mexican menus or outdoor dining.

1 envelope unflavored
    gelatin
1 cup cold water
1½ cups mashed avocados
½ cup Kraft Italian
    dressing

½ cup dairy sour cream
1 tablespoon finely
    chopped onion
Dash of hot pepper
    sauce
Mexi Bean Salad

Combine gelatin and cold water in saucepan; let stand 1 minute. Stir over medium heat until gelatin is dissolved; cool. Combine avocado, dressing, sour cream, onion and hot pepper sauce. Gradually add gelatin mixture to avocado mixture, mixing until blended. Pour into 3½-cup ring mold; chill until firm. Unmold; fill center with:

Mexi Bean Salad

1 16-oz. can kidney
    beans, drained
½ cup celery slices

¼ cup chopped sweet
    pickles
¼ cup Kraft French or
    garlic French dressing

Combine ingredients; mix lightly. Chill several hours or overnight. 6 to 8 servings

Heavenly Cheese Mold

Cheddar cheese and pineapple—a delightful combination.

1 8¼-oz. can crushed
    pineapple
1 3-oz. pkg. lemon
    flavored gelatin
1 cup boiling water
1 tablespoon lemon juice

1 cup (4 ozs.) shredded
    Kraft sharp cheddar
    cheese
1 cup heavy cream, stiffly
    whipped

Drain pineapple, reserving syrup. Dissolve gelatin in boiling water; add reserved syrup and enough cold water to measure ¾ cup. Stir in lemon juice. Chill until partially set; fold in pineapple, cheese and whipped cream. Pour into 1½-quart mold; chill until firm. Unmold. 6 to 8 servings

For best results, finely shred the cheese.

Salmon Mousse

A delicate pink, main-dish salad, particularly refreshing in warm summer weather.

2 envelopes unflavored
    gelatin
½ cup cold water
1 cup Kraft real
    mayonnaise
⅓ cup lemon juice
1 16-oz. can salmon,
    drained, flaked

1 cup finely chopped
    celery
¼ cup finely chopped
    green pepper
1 teaspoon finely
    chopped onion

Combine gelatin and water in saucepan; let stand 1 minute. Stir over medium heat until gelatin is dissolved; cool. Combine mayonnaise and lemon juice. Gradually add gelatin mixture to mayonnaise mixture, mixing until blended. Chill until partially set; fold in salmon and vegetables. Pour into 1-quart mold; chill until firm. Unmold. 6 to 8 servings

Use a fancy mold and serve the salad on bibb or leaf lettuce, surrounded by thinly sliced cucumber and ripe olives.

Mustard Mold

Colorful "condiment" mold, delicious with meat or poultry.

1 envelope unflavored
   gelatin
½ cup cold water
1 cup Kraft real
   mayonnaise

½ cup prepared mustard
¼ teaspoon salt
¼ teaspoon paprika
½ cup heavy cream,
   whipped

Combine gelatin and cold water in saucepan; let stand 1 minute. Stir over medium heat until gelatin is dissolved; cool. Combine mayonnaise, mustard and seasonings. Gradually add gelatin mixture to mayonnaise mixture, mixing until blended. Chill until partially set; fold in whipped cream. Pour into 1-quart mold; chill until firm. Unmold. 4 to 6 servings

Snowy Strawberry Mold

Definitely dramatic, this fresh strawberry mold with the creamy white cap is always a sensation—and a Kraft Kitchens' favorite.

1 11-oz. can mandarin
   orange segments
1 envelope unflavored
   gelatin
½ cup cold water
½ cup Miracle Whip
   salad dressing

1 3-oz. pkg. cream cheese
   * * *
2 3-oz. pkgs. strawberry
   flavored gelatin
2 cups boiling water
1½ cups cold water
1 cup strawberry slices

Drain orange segments, reserving ½ cup syrup. Combine unflavored gelatin and water in saucepan; let stand 1 minute. Stir over medium heat until gelatin is dissolved. Add syrup. Gradually add salad dressing to softened cream cheese, mixing until well blended. Stir in gelatin mixture. Pour into 1½-quart mold; chill until almost set.

Dissolve strawberry gelatin in boiling water; add cold water. Chill until partially set; fold in strawberries and orange segments. Pour over cream cheese layer; chill until firm. Unmold. 6 to 8 servings

Select a tall, fancy mold, and serve the salad on a footed plate surrounded by curly endive or lacy leaf lettuce.

Tomato Triumph Ring

A beautiful centerpiece for luncheon or supper buffets, this well-seasoned aspic has a refreshing middle layer of cream cheese and crisp fresh vegetables. Fill the center with chilled cooked shrimp.

2 envelopes unflavored
   gelatin
4 cups tomato juice
1 tablespoon grated
   onion
   Dash of salt and
   pepper
   *   *   *
1 envelope unflavored
   gelatin
¼ cup cold water

½ cup salad dressing or
   mayonnaise
1 8-oz. pkg. Philadelphia
   Brand cream cheese
1 cup finely chopped
   celery
1 tablespoon finely
   chopped green pepper
1 tablespoon finely
   chopped pimiento
1 teaspoon lemon juice
   Lettuce

Combine gelatin and 1 cup tomato juice; let stand 1 minute. Stir over medium heat until dissolved. Gradually add gelatin mixture to remaining tomato juice, onion and seasonings, mixing until blended. Pour half of tomato mixture into 6½-cup ring mold; chill until almost set.

Combine gelatin and cold water in saucepan; let stand 1 minute. Stir over medium heat until gelatin is dissolved; cool. Gradually add salad dressing to softened cream cheese, mixing until well blended. Add gelatin mixture, celery, green pepper, pimiento and lemon juice. Spread cream cheese mixture over tomato layer; chill until almost set. Pour remaining tomato mixture over cream cheese layer; chill until firm. Unmold; surround with lettuce. 10 to 12 servings

Dorothy Holland, director of the Kraft Kitchens, has one of the largest antique mold collections in the world. The intricate molds, made of silver, copper, Britannia metal (an alloy of tin, copper, and antimony) and salt-glaze stone and china, were originally used for frozen or refrigerated desserts, and steamed or baked puddings. The ancestry of many of the molds can be traced to the grand kitchens of British and European aristocracy.

Waldorf Crown Salad

This molded version of the famous Waldorf Salad has a very special dressing made with miniature marshmallows.

2 3-oz. pkgs. strawberry
    flavored gelatin
2 cups boiling water
1½ cups cold water
1 cup chopped apple

½ cup thin celery slices
¼ cup chopped walnuts
Lettuce
Fluffy Dressing

Dissolve gelatin in boiling water; add cold water. Chill until partially set; fold in apples, celery and nuts. Pour into 4½-cup ring mold; chill until firm. Unmold; surround with lettuce. Fill center with:

Fluffy Dressing

1 cup dairy sour cream
½ cup salad dressing or
    mayonnaise

1½ cups Kraft miniature
    marshmallows

Combine sour cream and salad dressing; mix well. Fold in marshmallows. 6 to 8 servings

Frozen Party Salad

A unique Kraft "classic" that was first featured in a 1934 ad.

1 cup Miracle Whip
    salad dressing
1 8-oz. pkg. cream cheese
1 20-oz. can pineapple
    chunks, drained
1 16-oz. can apricot
    halves, drained,
    quartered
½ cup chopped
    maraschino cherries

2 tablespoons
    confectioners' sugar
Few drops red food
    coloring
2 cups miniature
    marshmallows
1 cup heavy cream,
    whipped

Gradually add salad dressing to softened cream cheese, mixing until well blended. Stir in fruit, sugar and food coloring; fold in marshmallows and whipped cream. Pour into 9 × 5-inch loaf pan. Freeze. Unmold. 10 to 12 servings

Variation: Substitute one 16-oz. can peach slices, drained, for apricots.

Raspberry Freeze

A pretty, refreshing salad for summer entertaining.

¼ cup honey
1 8-oz. pkg. cream cheese
1 10-oz. pkg. frozen
  raspberries, partially
  thawed

1 cup banana slices
2 cups Kraft miniature
  marshmallows
1 cup heavy cream,
  whipped

Gradually add honey to softened cream cheese, mixing until well blended. Stir in fruit; fold in marshmallows and whipped cream. Pour into 9-inch square pan. Freeze. Place in refrigerator 30 minutes before serving. 9 servings

Variation: Pour mixture into ten 5-oz. paper cups; insert wooden sticks in center. Freeze.

Frozen salads should "temper" in the refrigerator before serving, so they thaw slightly for a more edible consistency.

Salsa

Colorful and crisp—great do-ahead for barbecues.

2 cups chopped tomatoes
1 cup caulifloweret slices
½ cup red onion rings
½ cup white onion rings
½ cup celery slices

¼ cup chopped green
  pepper
Catalina French or
  Kraft herb and garlic
  French dressing

Combine vegetables and enough dressing to moisten; toss lightly. Chill. 4 cups

Backyard Bean Salad

A kidney bean relish especially suited to casual meals, picnics and cookouts.

1 16-oz. can kidney
  beans, drained
2 hard-cooked eggs,
  chopped
½ cup chopped celery

⅓ cup Kraft thousand
  island dressing
1 tablespoon chopped
  onion
Salt and pepper

Combine kidney beans, eggs, celery, dressing and onion; toss lightly. Season to taste. Chill. 2½ cups

Garden Relish

A good snacking relish for calorie watchers. Keep this crunchy treat in the refrigerator, ready to satisfy the urge to munch.

2 cups chopped cabbage
⅓ cup chopped carrots
⅓ cup chopped green pepper
¼ cup chopped red onion

½ cup Kraft Italian, French or low calorie French dressing

Combine ingredients; toss lightly. Chill. 2¾ cups

Corn Relish

A midwestern specialty that's a Kraft "classic."

1 12-oz. can whole kernel corn, drained
½ cup chopped onion
⅓ cup chopped green pepper

¼ cup Catalina French dressing
2 tablespoons chopped pimiento

Combine ingredients; toss lightly. Chill. 2½ cups

This relish keeps for days, tightly covered in the refrigerator.

Simple Salad Combinations with Kraft Dressings

- Sliced tomatoes and finely chopped onion marinated in Miracle French dressing.

- Cucumbers and onion rings marinated in creamy garlic dressing or coleslaw dressing.

- Shredded iceberg lettuce, diced cheddar cheese, onion rings, tomato wedges and creamy cucumber dressing.

- Assorted greens, halved artichoke hearts, sliced pitted ripe olives, avocado wedges and caesar dressing.

- Iceberg lettuce chunks, sliced fresh mushrooms, tomato wedges, onion rings, and red wine vinegar and oil dressing or caesar dressing.

- Curly endive, orange slices, onion rings and Catalina French dressing.

The Kraft Story

1959–1964

The company's commitment to research and development began in the early years when J. L. Kraft's small scale research led to a revolutionary development—process cheese. By 1959, a fifteen-acre, modern research complex had been constructed in a Chicago suburb. Then, as today, a staff of skilled food scientists, technologists, and engineers concentrated their diverse training and expertise on a broad range of projects: innovative products; new or improved machinery and manufacturing methods; quality control; food safety; and nutritional analyses.

Two goals have guided Kraft's research endeavors through the years. The first goal is to develop high quality products that could be marketed at a fair price and that would exceed consumer expectations. A corresponding objective is to develop packaging that is attractive, protective, functional, sturdy, economical, and ecologically acceptable.

Research and Development has been a strong force in Kraft's product innovations: the patented process for Miracle Whip salad dressing; nutritional research that led to Velveeta pasteurized process cheese spread; whipped margarine in stick form; cheese in slices; natural cheese that cures in the package without molding.

The Kraft Kitchens have also played a significant role in product and packaging development by submitting prototype recipes and by testing and evaluating products from the consumer's viewpoint. All products are carefully analyzed for built-in service, ease of preparation, tolerance, and quality factors such as flavor, color, consistency, texture, and overall appetite appeal.

Kraft's continuing policy is to produce safe, nutritious, high-quality products that meet or exceed consumer expectations and that perform successfully in everyone's home.

Dressings and Sauces

Savory or sweet, dressings and sauces add special flavor or a touch of elegance to many basic foods. Early emigrés, especially those of French, English, or Italian origin, were well-versed in the art of "saucery." They knew that a well-seasoned sauce could skillfully stretch expensive meat dishes, disguise off-flavored foods, tenderize tough meat, and moisten stale cake or breads. Food was often scarce so it was seldom wasted. Then, as now, sauces were also valued for enhancing simple dishes, adding variety to everyday foods, and providing a flavorful binder or gravy for pot roast, stews, hash, or meat pies.

Today sauces, plain or fancy, have a prominent position in the daily menu. Seasoned tomato sauce on pasta, savory cheese sauce on fish or seafood, hollandaise on vegetables, hard sauce on fruitcake, and hot fudge topping on sundaes are just a few of the everyday favorites.

Salad dressings are relatively recent in America since few salads were served in the home until the 1930s. Convenience dressings appeared on the grocers' shelves paralleling the growing interest in salads.

Mayonnaise and salad dressings are easily varied. For example, simple additions to mayonnaise such as herbs, shredded cheese, crushed fruit, or preserves provide "personalized" dressings in minutes.

The following recipes are a few of our favorites to pique your imagination and add new interest to your menus.

Creamy Parmesan Dressing

A thick and creamy dressing for meat or vegetable salads, or a piquant sauce for vegetables such as peas, green beans, zucchini, baked potatoes.

½ cup mayonnaise	½ cup dairy sour cream
½ cup (2 ozs.) Kraft grated parmesan cheese	¼ cup milk

Combine ingredients; mix well. Chill. 1½ cups

Variation: For color, add chopped chives or parsley.

Honey Fruit Dressing

Tart, tropical dressing for fruit salads, particularly good with melon, peaches, grapes and oranges—serve for guest luncheons featuring main-dish salads.

¾ cup Kraft real mayonnaise	1 teaspoon grated lime rind
3 tablespoons honey	½ teaspoon celery seed
1 tablespoon lime juice	

Combine ingredients; mix well. Chill. 1 cup

Variation: Substitute poppy seed for celery seed.

Regency Dressing

Creamy herb dressing for meat or vegetables, or simple lettuce salads.

1 cup Kraft real mayonnaise	2 teaspoons cream style horseradish
¼ cup chopped parsley	Dash of salt
2 tablespoons chopped chives	

Combine ingredients; mix well. Chill. 1¼ cups

154

Marshmallow Dressing

Quick and creamy sweet dressing for fruit salads and gelatin molds.

½ cup salad dressing or mayonnaise

1 7-oz. jar Kraft marshmallow creme

Gradually add salad dressing to marshmallow creme, mixing until well blended. 1¼ cups

Peanut Butter Dressing

Family favorite for simple fruit salads made with apples, grapes, bananas and pears. Try it with Waldorf Salad!

¼ cup peanut butter
3 tablespoons honey

1 cup Kraft real mayonnaise
1 tablespoon milk

Combine peanut butter and honey, mixing until well blended. Add mayonnaise and milk; mix well. Chill. 1½ cups

Louis Dressing

Generally associated with crabmeat salads or appetizers, this is also delicious with vegetables or meat salads.

½ cup Kraft real mayonnaise
½ cup chili sauce

½ teaspoon Worcestershire sauce

Combine ingredients; mix well. Chill. 1 cup

Spanish Dressing

A quick, tangy dressing to serve over assorted greens.

1 8-oz. bottle Kraft oil and vinegar dressing
2 tablespoons chopped stuffed green olives

1 tablespoon green onion slices

Combine ingredients in pint jar. Cover; shake well. Chill. Shake well before serving. 1¼ cups

Sherbet Dressing

Something special for fruit salads and gelatin molds, this colorful, fluffy dressing is terrific for parties.

1 cup raspberry,
pineapple, orange or
lime sherbet, softened

1 cup Kraft real
mayonnaise

Combine ingredients; mix well. Chill. 2 cups

Roquefort Dressing Supreme

A Kraft "classic" for epicurean tastes, this marvelous blend of cream cheese and chunky Roquefort is perfect for meat and vegetable salads.

1 8-oz. pkg. Philadelphia
Brand cream cheese
¾ cup (3 ozs.) Roquefort
cheese
¾ cup milk
¼ cup mayonnaise
3 tablespoons lemon
juice

2 tablespoons chopped
chives
1 teaspoon
Worcestershire sauce
Dash of hot pepper
sauce

Combine softened cream cheese and Roquefort cheese, mixing until well blended. Add remaining ingredients; mix well. Chill. 2½ cups

Coliseum Dressing

Spoon this dressing over lettuce wedges—simple but special.

1 cup Kraft real
mayonnaise
¼ cup caesar dressing

2 tablespoons chopped
ripe olives

Combined ingredients; mix well. Chill. 1¼ cups

Brandy Pecan Sauce

Quick-easy praline sauce for sundaes, parfaits and cheese-cake. Perfect hurry-up dessert—this sauce on pound cake à la mode.

1 12-oz. jar Kraft
    artificially flavored
    butterscotch topping

½ cup chopped pecans
¼ cup margarine
¼ cup brandy

Heat topping, nuts and margarine, stirring occasionally. Add brandy. Cool. 2 cups

Caramel Sauce

A Kraft "classic" since the mid-1930s, when Kraft caramels were first introduced. A convenience version, Kraft caramel topping, was later developed in answer to consumer requests.

28 Kraft caramels   ⅓ cup water

Melt caramels with water in saucepan over low heat. Stir frequently until sauce is smooth. ¾ cup

Variations: Add ¼ cup chopped pecans, walnuts or peanuts. Reduce water to ¼ cup; add 1 tablespoon rum or brandy.

Both this sauce and Kraft caramel topping are delicious on almost any ice cream. Use them too on baked apples, warm pies—pear, apple or peach—and on crisps and cobblers of any kind.

Creamy Dill Sauce

Refreshing sauce for green beans, asparagus, broiled tomatoes, baked ham or fish—especially good on salmon.

½ cup Kraft real
    mayonnaise
½ cup dairy sour cream

⅓ cup drained shredded
    cucumber
½ teaspoon dill weed

Combine ingredients; mix well. Chill. 1¼ cups

To maintain the pace of "live" television commercials, two matched pairs of hands worked in relays before two cameras. The result was a smoothly executed sequence which was perceived as the action of one camera and one pair of hands.

Fluffy Horseradish Sauce

Pungent sauce for hot or cold meats. Try it on vegetables such as green beans, broccoli and asparagus.

1 cup Kraft real
   mayonnaise
¼ cup cream style
   horseradish

½ cup heavy cream,
   whipped

Combine mayonnaise and horseradish; mix well. Fold in whipped cream. Chill. 1½ cups

Golden Sauce

Simple, easy to make and very good, this has been a basic sauce in homes throughout the country since the mid-1930s.

½ lb. Velveeta process
   cheese spread, cubed

¼ cup milk

Heat cheese spread and milk over low heat; stir until smooth. 1 cup

Most commonly used over hot cooked vegetables, but also excellent over sandwiches, meat, fish and omelets, or in casseroles and main dishes.

Gourmet Sauce

Unique two-cheese sauce for vegetables, meats and fish.

1 8-oz. pkg. cream
   cheese, cubed
½ cup milk

¼ cup (1 oz.) Kraft grated
   parmesan cheese
¼ teaspoon garlic salt

Heat cream cheese and milk over low heat; stir until smooth. Blend in remaining ingredients. 1¾ cups

Variations: Add sliced green onions, chopped parsley or chives, or mushrooms.

Tolerance testing is an important function of the Kraft Kitchens. In order to be acceptable, products must be adaptable to minor variations in cooking time and temperature, gas or electric heat, type of equipment and human error.

Cheddar Cheese Sauce

A Kraft "classic" from the 1920s—superb and versatile.

2 tablespoons margarine
2 tablespoons flour
1 cup milk
¼ teaspoon salt
Dash of cayenne

Dash of dry mustard
1 cup (4 ozs.) shredded
Cracker Barrel sharp
cheddar cheese

Make a white sauce with margarine, flour, milk and seasonings. Add cheese; stir until melted. 1⅓ cups

Use this great sauce any number of ways—over toast; over hot ham, chicken, egg or tomato sandwiches; over hot cooked vegetables, rice or pasta; and in casseroles and main dishes.

Hard Sauce

Traditional sauce for steamed or baked puddings, delicious on warm mince or raisin pies or as a topper for fruit cake.

½ cup Parkay margarine
1 teaspoon vanilla

2 cups sifted
confectioners' sugar

Cream margarine; blend in vanilla. Add sugar, beating until light and fluffy. 1⅓ cups

Variations: Substitute 1 tablespoon rum or brandy for the vanilla; blend in additional sugar for the desired consistency.

"Philly" Chocolate Sauce

A deliciously rich chocolate sauce for ice cream, cake or your favorite fruit.

1 8-oz. pkg. Philadelphia
Brand cream cheese
⅓ cup milk
2 1-oz. squares
unsweetened chocolate

2 cups sifted
confectioner's sugar
1 teaspoon vanilla

Heat cream cheese, milk and chocolate over low heat; stir until smooth. Blend in remaining ingredients. 2 cups

This sauce can be served hot or cold, and can be reheated.

Holiday Sauce

Makes a festive sundae sauce, delicious too on cheesecake or everybody's favorite—apple pie à la mode.

1 cup ready-to-use mincemeat	½ cup Kraft orange marmalade
	¼ cup margarine

Heat ingredients, stirring occasionally. Serve warm over ice cream. 1½ cups

Variation: Add 1 or 2 tablespoons of rum or brandy.

Mornay Sauce

Thick, rich cheese sauce that resembles fondue—compatible with almost any vegetable, particularly appealing over hot chicken, turkey or ham sandwiches served open-style.

¼ cup margarine	1 cup (4 ozs.) shredded Kraft aged Swiss cheese
¼ cup flour	
2 cups milk	
½ teaspoon salt	¼ cup (1 oz.) grated parmesan cheese
Dash of pepper	

Make a white sauce with margarine, flour, milk and seasonings. Add Swiss and parmesan cheese; stir until melted. 2½ cups

"Philly" Hard Sauce

Variation on an old favorite—smooth textured, with a mild brandy flavor.

1 3-oz. pkg. Philadelphia Brand cream cheese	Dash of salt
1 teaspoon brandy flavoring	2½ cups sifted confectioners' sugar

Combine softened cream cheese, flavoring and salt, mixing until well blended. Add sugar, beating until light and fluffy. 1 cup

Delicious on bread pudding, fruitcake, steamed puddings or warm fruit pies.

Royal Mustard Sauce

Beautifully blended creamy sauce for hot or cold meats, fish and poultry.

1 cup Miracle Whip
  salad dressing
¼ cup milk
1 tablespoon prepared
  mustard

½ teaspoon
  Worcestershire sauce
½ teaspoon salt

Combine ingredients; mix well. 1⅓ cups

For entertaining, serve Royal Mustard Sauce with baked ham, salmon steaks or a platter of assorted cold meats.

Tarragon Sauce

A superior but easy sauce for hot or cold fish, ham, chicken and seafood—particularly good on seafood salads.

⅔ cup Kraft real
  mayonnaise
⅔ cup dairy sour cream
2 tablespoons green
  onion slices
1 teaspoon prepared
  mustard

½ teaspoon salt
¼ teaspoon tarragon
  leaves, crushed
Dash of cayenne

Combine ingredients; mix well. Chill. 1⅓ cups

Tartar Sauce

Excellent, flavorful sauce for baked, broiled or fried fish, fish sticks, fish sandwiches—also delicious with ham!

1 cup Kraft real
  mayonnaise
2 tablespoons chopped
  dill pickle
1 tablespoon chopped
  capers

1 tablespoon chopped
  parsley
1 tablespoon chopped
  onion
1 tablespoon chopped
  pimiento

Combine ingredients; mix well. Chill. 1¼ cups

163

The Kraft Story

1965–1972

This era was remarkable for packaging research and innovations, which have always been major company priorities. Kraft packaging must protect product quality from the time of manufacture to the time of recommended use. To achieve this goal, food scientists and engineers in our research laboratories continually study, analyze, and develop new materials, types of packaging, and production methods. Each product has specific packaging requirements.

Several significant innovations evolved during the latter 1960s. Kraft American Singles pasteurized process cheese food slices were introduced in 1965. The slices were individually wrapped in a plastic wrap then overwrapped together in 12-ounce packages to prevent drying which had been a problem for consumers who only used one or two slices at a time. This sliced cheese product is now an established leader in the cheese industry.

Squeeze Parkay margarine in a soft flexible bottle followed in 1969. The margarine had to be thin enough at refrigerator temperature to pass through a very small spout, yet be sufficiently thick to stay on foods such as corn on the cob. The spout had to be the correct size or it could plug. Once it was marketed, the product answered consumer expectations for a margarine that could be dispensed with ease on popcorn, waffles, pancakes, toast, chicken, fish, and similar foods.

Squeez-A-Snak process cheese spread was also introduced in 1969 as Kraft's alternative to cheese spreads in aerosol cans. The soft plastic container, which resembles a short fat sausage, has an opening in the middle with a plastic lid for reclosing after use. When the tube is compressed, the cheese spread is readily dispensed in a decorative design. Squeez-A-Snak is a high-quality, economical cheese spread which is stable at room temperature and can be dispensed easily. It was an instant success!

Another response to consumer requests was the new rigid box for Philadelphia Brand cream cheese. The original foil wrap was easily crushed, therefore the product was often damaged before it reached the home. The new box was more durable, provided better protection, and kept the cream cheese fresher for a longer period. It also required twelve percent less packaging material because it eliminated the need for additional packaging during shipping.

Innovations like these are a frequent occurrence at Kraft as scientists seek new ways to protect products, respond to consumers, and reduce costs.

Vegetables

America the bountiful is an apt phrase when describing the nation's vast and varied supply of vegetables. Every region has its specialties—pumpkin, squash, beans, potatoes, beets, and wild rice in the Northeast; turnips, mustard greens, collard, kale, watercress, yams, and okra in the South; corn, beans, squash, and soy beans in the Midwest; tomatoes, asparagus, chili peppers, dried beans, and lettuce in the West. Corn is probably the most uniquely American and widely grown vegetable.

The Indians were excellent farmers and taught the early settlers new and economical ways to cultivate vegetables. Corn was planted in rows and surrounded by other vegetables. The cornstalks acted as supports for the climbing vegetables.

Vegetables, more than other foods, add variety, color, texture and flavor to meals. They are also a versatile food since they can be chopped, diced, sliced, cubed, simmered, sautéed, French fried, stir-fried, baked, creamed, or marinated.

A few precautions are necessary in selecting, storing, and preparing fresh vegetables. Choose vegetables that are blemish-free and at peak condition. Carefully wash (but do not soak) and refrigerate them in plastic bags or in the hydrator compartment. Root vegetables are the exception and should be stored, unwashed, in a cool, dark, and well-ventilated area.

The recipes in this chapter offer many "unusual" ways of preparing "usual" vegetables.

Cauliflower Amandine

A full head of cauliflower topped with golden Velveeta sauce and toasted almonds makes a grand display for attractive buffet service.

½ lb. Velveeta process
  cheese spread, sliced
¼ cup milk

1 head cauliflower,
  cooked
Sliced almonds, toasted

Heat cheese spread and milk over low heat; stir until smooth. Pour sauce over cauliflower; sprinkle with nuts. 3 to 4 servings

Zucchini Sticks Au Gratin

New way with an old favorite—parmesan makes the flavor difference.

4 medium zucchini, cut
  into julienne sticks
¼ cup Squeeze Parkay
  margarine

Salt and pepper
½ cup dry bread crumbs
2 tablespoons grated
  parmesan cheese

Stir-fry zucchini in margarine until crisp-tender. Season to taste. Stir in combined crumbs and cheese; heat thoroughly. 4 to 6 servings

Cheddar-Corn Fritters

A traditional southern favorite, these fritters are delicious with chicken, turkey or ham. Be prepared to double the recipe!

1¼ cups flour
1 teaspoon baking
  powder
1 teaspoon salt
1 cup (4 ozs.) shredded
  Kraft sharp cheddar
  cheese

½ cup milk
1 egg, beaten
2 tablespoons margarine,
  melted
1 12-oz. can whole kernel
  corn, drained
Oil

Combine dry ingredients; stir in cheese. Add milk, egg and margarine; mix well. Fold in corn. Drop rounded tablespoon-fuls of dough into deep hot oil, 375°. Fry 3 to 4 minutes or until golden brown. Drain. Serve warm. Approximately 1½ dozen

Cheese and Rice Croquettes

This recipe appeared in a Kraft ad in the Saturday Evening Post in 1927. Croquettes were often served with a spicy tomato sauce, or with vegetables such as peas, asparagus, carrots, broccoli.

¼ cup margarine
⅓ cup flour
1 cup milk
¼ teaspoon salt
1 cup (4 ozs.) shredded
   Deluxe Choice•Old
   English process
   American cheese

2 cups cooked rice
¾ cup dry bread crumbs
1 egg, beaten
2 tablespoons water

Make a white sauce with margarine, flour, milk and salt. Add cheese; stir until melted. Cool; mix with rice. For each serving, form ⅓ cup rice mixture into cone-shaped croquette. Coat with crumbs; dip in combined egg and water. Coat again with crumbs. Fry in deep hot oil, 375°, until golden brown. 8 servings

Cinnamon Baked Squash

Spicy accompaniment for baked ham, roast pork or any style of chicken. Since acorn squash is hearty, smaller servings will satisfy children.

3 acorn squash, halved,
   seeded
Cinnamon

⅓ cup Squeeze Parkay
   margarine
⅓ cup packed brown
   sugar

Place squash in baking dish, cut side down. Bake at 400°, 30 minutes. Turn squash cut side up. Sprinkle with cinnamon; brush with combined margarine and sugar. Fill centers of squash with remaining margarine mixture; continue baking 30 minutes. 6 servings

To Microcook: Prick whole squash with fork. Microcook whole squash 18 minutes or until tender, rearranging three times; let stand 5 minutes. Cut in half; remove seeds. Place squash in baking dish, cut side up. Sprinkle with cinnamon; brush with combined margarine and sugar. Fill centers of squash with margarine mixture. Microcook 2 minutes.

Mallow-Whipt Sweet Potatoes

Golden sweet potato casserole, mildly flavored with orange juice and marshmallows.

4 cups hot mashed sweet
    potatoes
¼ cup margarine
¼ cup orange juice

½ teaspoon salt
Kraft miniature
    marshmallows

Combine sweet potatoes, margarine, orange juice and salt. Add 1 cup marshmallows; beat until fluffy. Spoon into 1½-quart casserole. Bake at 350°, 20 minutes. Sprinkle with additional marshmallows; broil until lightly browned. 6 servings

Cheese Stuffed Potatoes

This twice-baked potato recipe first appeared in 1923 issues of Ladies Home Journal and Good Housekeeping magazines. For variety, add sliced green onions, chopped chives or parsley, or crisp bacon.

4 large baked potatoes
1 cup (4 ozs.) shredded
    Deluxe Choice
    process American
    cheese

⅓ cup milk
¼ cup margarine
½ teaspoon salt
Paprika

Slice potatoes in half lengthwise; scoop out centers, leaving ⅛-inch shell. Heat cheese, milk and margarine over low heat; stir until smooth. Combine with potato and salt; beat until fluffy. Fill shells; sprinkle with paprika. Place on cookie sheet. Bake at 375°, 25 minutes. 8 servings

To Make Ahead: Prepare recipe as directed, except for baking. Wrap securely; freeze. Unwrap; bake at 375°, for 45 minutes.

To Microcook: Slice potatoes in half lengthwise; scoop out centers, leaving ⅛-inch shell. Microcook cheese, milk and margarine 1½ minutes; stir until smooth. Combine with potato and salt; beat until fluffy. Fill shells; sprinkle with paprika. Place in baking dish. Microcook 7 minutes, turning dish once.

Country Scallop

Colorful version of scalloped cabbage with rich cheddar sauce. Larger servings of this casserole are hearty enough for a meatless main dish.

6 cups chopped cabbage
2 cups carrot slices
⅓ cup margarine, melted
2 tablespoons flour
1 cup milk
¼ teaspoon dry mustard

¼ teaspoon paprika
1½ cups (6 ozs.) shredded Kraft sharp cheddar cheese
1½ cups soft bread crumbs

Combine cabbage and carrots in 11¾ × 7½-inch baking dish. Make a white sauce with 2 tablespoons margarine, flour, milk and seasonings. Add cheese; stir until melted. Pour sauce over vegetables. Top with bread crumbs tossed with remaining margarine. Bake at 350°, 55 to 60 minutes. 8 servings

Creamy Potato Puff

Cream cheese-potato dish, handsome enough for the most special occasion.

4 cups hot mashed potatoes
1 8-oz. pkg. Philadelphia Brand cream cheese
1 egg, beaten

⅓ cup finely chopped onion
¼ cup chopped pimiento
1 teaspoon salt
Dash of pepper

Combine potatoes and cream cheese, mixing until well blended. Add remaining ingredients; mix well. Spoon into 1½-quart casserole. Bake at 350°, 40 minutes. 6 to 8 servings

Variations: Add finely chopped green pepper, shredded carrot or grated parmesan cheese. Sprinkle with crumbled crisply cooked bacon.

Since the beginning of its television involvement, Kraft has brought drama, mystery, comedy, fantasy, song, and dance to millions of Americans. The list of well-known entertainers who have performed on Kraft programs includes Milton Berle, Perry Como, Andy Williams, and John Davidson.

Creole Corn

Popular skillet vegetable for barbecues and casual dinners. Fresh corn and tomatoes can be used when available.

½ cup chopped onion
¼ cup margarine
¼ cup flour
   Dash of pepper
1 17-oz. can whole kernel
   corn, undrained

1 16-oz. can tomatoes,
   drained
¼ lb. Velveeta process
   cheese spread, cubed

Sauté onion in margarine; blend in flour and pepper. Stir in corn and tomatoes; cook, stirring constantly, until thickened. Add cheese spread; stir until melted. 8 servings

Georgian Spinach Soufflé

A feature attraction for guest dinners or a colorful main dish for luncheons—like all soufflés, it must go directly from oven to table.

¼ cup margarine
¼ cup flour
¾ cup milk
   Dash of pepper
½ lb. Velveeta process
   cheese spread, cubed
1 10-oz. pkg. frozen
   chopped spinach,
   cooked, well-drained

6 crisply cooked bacon
   slices, crumbled
1 tablespoon finely
   chopped onion
4 eggs, separated
¼ teaspoon cream of
   tartar

Make a white sauce with margarine, flour, milk and pepper. Add cheese spread; stir until melted. Remove from heat. Stir in spinach, bacon and onion. Gradually add slightly beaten egg yolks; cool. Beat egg whites and cream of tartar until stiff peaks form. Fold spinach mixture into egg whites; pour into 2-quart soufflé dish. Bake at 325°, 1 hour. Serve immediately. 8 servings

This comment from one viewer is a testimonial for the effectiveness of Kraft commercials —"I don't watch the show, but I do watch the commercials. They give me ideas I don't want to miss."

Gourmet Green Beans

Bacon and onion for seasoning, Cheez Whiz as an instant sauce.

6 bacon slices
¼ cup chopped onion
2 9-oz. pkgs. frozen cut green beans, cooked, drained

1 8-oz. jar Cheez Whiz process cheese spread
1 4-oz. can mushrooms, drained

Fry bacon until crisp; drain. Crumble bacon. Sauté onion. Add bacon and remaining ingredients. Heat thoroughly, stirring occasionally. 6 to 8 servings

Oriental Vegetables

So easy, so elegant! Vegetables prepared the oriental way—diagonally cut and stir-fried—retain their fresh color and crisp texture.

2 cups diagonally cut carrot slices
1 cup diagonally cut celery slices
½ cup thin green pepper strips

2 tablespoons Squeeze Parkay margarine
Salt and pepper
Sesame seeds, toasted

Stir-fry vegetables in margarine until crisp-tender. Season to taste. Sprinkle with sesame seeds. 4 servings

Picnic Bean Treat

Great for any cookout—increase the recipe for a crowd.

1 16-oz. can baked beans
1 16-oz. can kidney beans, drained
½ cup Kraft barbecue sauce

½ cup onion rings
¼ cup chopped dill pickle

Combine ingredients; mix lightly. Cover; simmer 20 minutes. 6 to 8 servings

Potatoes Elegante

Potatoes never tasted so good or looked so inviting! Thinly sliced and oven baked to a delicate brown, this upside-down dish is a variation of the French specialty, Potatoes Anna.

6 medium potatoes,
  peeled, thinly sliced
⅓ cup Squeeze Parkay
  margarine

1 cup (4 ozs.) Kraft
  grated parmesan
  cheese

Rinse potatoes; dry thoroughly. Brush 1 tablespoon margarine on bottom and sides of 9-inch pie plate; sprinkle with 1 tablespoon cheese. Toss potatoes with remaining margarine. Layer half of potatoes on bottom and sides of pie plate; sprinkle with cheese. Repeat layers. Bake at 400°, 1 hour or until potatoes are tender. Invert immediately onto serving plate. 4 to 6 servings

Herb Rice

A colorful rice specialty—uniquely seasoned with dill—that can be prepared in advance and reheated just before serving.

1 cup thinly sliced
  carrots
1 cup chopped onion
¼ cup Parkay margarine
3 cups water
2 cups rice

2 teaspoons salt
½ teaspoon dill weed
  Dash of pepper
2 tablespoons chopped
  parsley

Sauté carrots and onion in margarine 5 minutes, stirring occasionally. Add water, rice, salt, dill weed and pepper; bring to a boil. Cover; simmer 20 to 25 minutes or until rice is tender. Stir in parsley. 8 to 10 servings

During the late 1960s, Kraft expanded its consumer and nutrition education programs to include multi-media teaching kits and free-loan films intended for classroom education, television, civic organizations, and professional associations. At present, four kits and two free-loan films are in distribution.

Ratatouille

This flavorful vegetable mélange originated in Provence, France, and is becoming increasingly popular in the United States. Can be made in advance—serve cold or reheated.

2 cups zucchini slices	½ cup red onion slices
2 cups cubed peeled eggplant	½ cup Catalina French dressing
1 green pepper, cut into strips	2 cups cherry tomatoes

Combine ingredients, except tomatoes, in skillet. Cover; cook over low heat 10 minutes. Stir in tomatoes; heat. Serve hot or cold. 6 servings

In the 1920s, long before ecology was an issue, Kraft had what may have been the first mobile environmental control laboratory to monitor plant discharges. More recently, a complete "environmental audit" of all Kraft locations is a continuing program to detect and correct potential problems.

Potato Pancakes

Long-time favorite in ethnic neighborhoods—delicious topped with applesauce or preserves. Potato pancakes can also be served as an appealing appetizer, with sour cream and caviar.

1 egg, beaten	2 cups shredded potatoes, rinsed, well-drained
2 tablespoons flour	
2 tablespoons grated onion	
¼ teaspoon salt	½ cup Squeeze Parkay margarine

Combine egg, flour, onion and salt; mix well. Stir in potatoes. Heat margarine in skillet. For each pancake, fry ¼ cup mixture until crisp and golden brown on both sides. 8 pancakes

Skillet Potatoes Au Gratin

Colorful and attractive, a hearty potato dish flavored with bacon and golden cheddar cheese.

6 bacon slices, chopped
½ cup chopped onion
4 cups cooked potato
   slices
2 cups (8 ozs.) shredded
   Kraft sharp cheddar
   cheese

1 10-oz. pkg. frozen peas,
   cooked, drained
1 cup milk
½ cup salad dressing or
   mayonnaise

Fry bacon until crisp; drain. Sauté onion. Add bacon, potatoes, ½ cup cheese and remaining ingredients. Heat thoroughly. Top with remaining cheese. 8 servings

Variations: Substitute sliced carrots, zucchini, green beans or celery for peas. For a main dish, omit bacon and add 2 cups chopped ham or sliced frankfurters.

In 1969, National Dairy Products Corporation, of which Kraft Foods was a division, was renamed Kraftco Corporation.

Toasty Noodle 'n Vegetable Pie

Unique and definitely special, this vegetable custard pie can serve as a hearty accompaniment or a meatless main dish.

1 pkg. Kraft egg noodle
   and cheese dinner
1 10-oz. pkg. frozen
   chopped broccoli,
   partially thawed
½ cup milk
2 eggs, beaten
¼ cup finely chopped
   onion

1 teaspoon salt
Dash of pepper
1½ cups soft white bread
   cubes
2 tablespoons Squeeze
   Parkay margarine

Prepare dinner as directed on package. Add broccoli, milk, eggs, onion and seasonings; mix well. Spoon into 9-inch pie plate. Top with bread cubes tossed with margarine. Bake at 350°, 40 minutes. Let stand 5 minutes. 8 servings

Southern-Style Sweet Potatoes

Old-fashioned candied sweet potatoes with fluffy marshmallow topping.

2 17-oz. cans sweet potato halves, drained	¼ cup margarine Kraft miniature marshmallows
½ cup packed brown sugar	

Drain sweet potatoes, reserving 2 tablespoons syrup. Combine syrup, sugar and margarine in saucepan; bring to boil. Boil 5 minutes, stirring constantly. Combine with potatoes in 1-quart casserole. Bake at 375°, 30 minutes, basting occasionally. Sprinkle with marshmallows; broil until lightly browned. 6 servings

For variety, sprinkle with toasted pecan halves or slivered almonds.

Savory Spinach Casserole

A marvelous cream cheese and parmesan topping highlights this layered spinach casserole.

1 8-oz. pkg. Philadelphia Brand cream cheese	⅓ cup grated parmesan cheese
¼ cup milk	
2 10-oz. pkgs. frozen chopped spinach, cooked, drained	

Combine softened cream cheese and milk, mixing until well blended. Place spinach in 1-quart casserole; top with cream cheese mixture. Sprinkle with parmesan cheese. Bake at 350°, 20 minutes. 4 to 6 servings

In 1970, Kraft established the Hostess Awards competition in conjunction with the America's Junior Miss program. Through this party planning activity, Kraft encourages awareness of wholesome food, nutrition, and menu planning among the participants.

The Kraft Story

1973–1978

The seventies have witnessed several significant achievements in structural reorganization, consumer commitments, and product innovations. In 1976, Kraftco Corporation consolidated its divisions into a single operating company with a new name—Kraft, Inc. For greater efficiency and utilization of all corporate resources, business is now conducted through groups devoted to specific responsibilities.

Today consumers demand more than quality products at a fair price. They are now interested in more detailed product and company information. In response, Kraft has expanded its communication efforts and reaffirmed several of its consumer commitments.

In 1974, an information program entitled CONSUMER'S RIGHT TO KNOW was initiated. The program utilizes newsletters, booklets, radio and television announcements, news releases, and ads to reach educators, communicators, and the general public with information about current issues and concerns—food safety, nutrition, additives, government regulations, economics, product innovations, and similar topics.

Kraft recently reaffirmed, publicly, its long-standing policy of not advertising on any radio or television program associated with excessive sex, shock, or violence, or which requires a parental discretion advisory. Over the years, Kraft has consistently sponsored wholesome entertainment for the entire family on radio and television.

A Nutrition Task Force was established in 1976, to direct Kraft's diverse nutrition programs and to formalize Kraft's policy with respect to nutrition aspects of its products.

Two major product innovations have been introduced in the last few years. Light n' Lively pasteurized process cheese product in several varieties is an all-dairy product line that has less than half the fat of regular American cheese, fewer calories, and about the same amount of protein. Golden Image imitation cheese products were test marketed in 1976. The product is labeled "imitation" because the butterfat of natural cheese is replaced largely by corn oil.

Kraft has changed with the times, but its basic philosophy has remained the same. The principle of learning what consumers expect and need and responding with the best value possible is as sound today as it was nearly three generations ago.

Desserts

Is there an American who does not like desserts? We are a country of dessert buffs. Whether it is a memorable masterpiece or a simple fruit dessert, most of us believe that dinner should have a sweet finale.

Due to our diverse cultural heritage, the traditional American cuisine boasts the greatest selection of desserts of any country. We inherited pies from the English; cookies from the Scandinavians and Germans; ice cream and frozen desserts from the Italians and French; cheesecakes from the Germans; and soufflés from the French—just to name a few! In our typically American way, we have adapted the recipes, expanded the varieties, and substituted native ingredients until the new versions bear only a vague resemblance to the original. (This is probably why we have inaccurate maxims such as, "American as apple pie"—which is really British.)

Of course, the U.S. does have its originals—strawberry shortcake, brownies, sugar cookies, layer cake, Indian pudding, apple crisp, and upside-down cake.

Over a period of fifty years, Kraft's list of "most requested" recipes has grown steadily. Many of the "classics" are presented here—Hollywood Cheesecake, Miracle Whip Chocolate Cake, Tennessee Jam Cake, Brown-Eyed Susans, Caramel Pecan Pie, Fantasy Fudge, Strawberry Cream Cheese Pie. They range from elegant to simple and many include do-ahead convenience preparation. We think all of them are special!

Banana Crunch Cake

A great cake for informal parties and picnics.

⅔ cup Parkay margarine
1⅔ cups sugar
3 eggs
1¼ cups mashed bananas
2¼ cups flour

1¼ teaspoons baking powder
1¼ teaspoons soda
1 teaspoon salt
⅔ cup buttermilk
Crunchy Topping

Cream margarine and sugar until light and fluffy. Blend in eggs and bananas. Add combined dry ingredients to creamed mixture alternately with buttermilk, mixing well after each addition. Pour into greased and floured 13 × 9-inch baking pan. Bake at 350°, 45 to 50 minutes. Spread Crunchy Topping over warm cake; broil until bubbly and golden brown.

Crunchy Topping: Combine ¾ cup packed brown sugar, ½ cup chopped pecans, one 3½-oz. can flaked coconut, ⅓ cup Parkay margarine, softened, and 2 tablespoons milk.

Cherry Orchard Cake

Old-fashioned cherry nut cake with a marmalade topping.

1 16-oz. can pitted sour cherries
½ cup margarine
1 cup sugar
2 eggs
1 teaspoon vanilla
1¾ cups flour
2 teaspoons baking powder

½ teaspoon salt
½ cup milk
½ cup chopped walnuts
* * *
½ cup sugar
1 tablespoon cornstarch
½ cup Kraft orange marmalade

Drain cherries, reserving syrup. Cream margarine and sugar. Blend in eggs and vanilla. Add combined 1½ cups flour, baking powder and salt alternately with milk, mixing well after each addition. Combine cherries and nuts with remaining flour; fold into batter. Pour into greased and floured 9-inch square pan. Bake at 350°, 50 to 55 minutes.

Combine sugar and cornstarch in saucepan; gradually add reserved syrup with enough water to measure 1 cup. Bring to boil, stirring constantly. Cook over medium heat until mixture is clear and thickened. Stir in marmalade. Serve with cake.

Easy Upside-Down Cake

A modern version of a traditional favorite—updated for convenience with Squeeze Parkay margarine, preserves and cake mix. So easy and so delicious!

1 20-oz. can sliced pineapple	1 10-oz. jar Kraft strawberry or apricot preserves
¼ cup Squeeze Parkay margarine	1 pkg. two layer yellow cake mix
10 pecan halves	

Thoroughly drain pineapple slices, reserving ¼ cup syrup. Cover bottom of 13 × 9-inch baking pan with margarine. Arrange pineapple and nuts in pan. Combine reserved syrup and preserves; spoon over pineapple. Prepare cake mix as directed on package. Pour batter over preserves mixture. Bake at 350°, 40 to 45 minutes. Immediately invert on serving platter.

Heidelberg Chocolate Cake

A light, fine-textured cake made with sweet German chocolate and a creamy coconut-pecan topping—serve this on special occasions.

1 cup Parkay margarine	2¼ cups flour
1⅔ cups sugar	2 teaspoons baking powder
4 eggs, separated	½ teaspoon salt
1 4-oz. pkg. sweet chocolate, melted	1¼ cups milk
1 teaspoon vanilla	Coconut Topping

Cream margarine and sugar until light and fluffy. Blend in egg yolks, chocolate and vanilla. Add combined dry ingredients to creamed mixture alternately with milk, mixing well after each addition. Fold in stiffly beaten egg whites. Pour into greased and floured 10-inch tube pan. Bake at 350°, 1 hour and 10 to 15 minutes. Cool 10 minutes; remove from pan. Frost top with:

Coconut Topping: In saucepan, combine ¼ cup each Parkay margarine, packed brown sugar and milk with 1 beaten egg. Cook over low heat, stirring constantly, until thickened. Stir in 1 cup each chopped pecans and flaked coconut and 1 teaspoon vanilla.

"Philly" Pound Cake

A Kraft "classic" since the 1930s.

1 8-oz. pkg. Philadelphia
    Brand cream cheese
¾ cup margarine
1½ cups sugar
1½ teaspoons vanilla

4 eggs
2 cups sifted cake flour
1½ teaspoons baking
    powder

Combine softened cream cheese, margarine, sugar and vanilla, mixing until well blended. Add eggs; mix at low speed on electric mixer until blended. Gradually add flour sifted with baking powder, mixing at low speed until blended. Pour into greased and floured 9 × 5-inch loaf pan. Bake at 325°, 1 hour and 20 minutes. Cool 5 minutes; remove from pan. Sprinkle with confectioners' sugar, if desired.

Tennessee Jam Cake

A southern tradition, handed down through generations.

1 cup margarine
1½ cups granulated sugar
1 10-oz. jar Kraft
    strawberry, raspberry
    or blackberry
    preserves
4 eggs
2½ cups flour

1 teaspoon soda
1 teaspoon nutmeg
1 teaspoon cinnamon
1 teaspoon cloves
¼ teaspoon salt
1 cup buttermilk
1½ cups chopped pecans
    Brown Sugar Frosting
    Confectioners' sugar

Cream margarine and granulated sugar until light and fluffy. Blend in preserves and eggs. Add combined dry ingredients to creamed mixture alternately with buttermilk, mixing well after each addition. Stir in nuts. Pour into three greased and floured 9-inch layer pans. Bake at 350°, 30 to 35 minutes. Cool 10 minutes; remove from pans. Fill and frost sides with Brown Sugar Frosting. Sift confectioners' sugar over top of cake.

Brown Sugar Frosting: Combine 1 cup packed brown sugar, ½ cup margarine and ¼ cup milk; bring to boil, stirring constantly. Remove from heat; cool 10 minutes. Gradually add 3 cups sifted confectioners' sugar, beating until well blended.

Miracle Whip Chocolate Cake

Developed during World War II, when many foods were rationed, this cake has topped the list of most requested recipes for over 30 years.

1 cup Miracle Whip
   salad dressing
1 cup sugar
1 teaspoon vanilla
2¼ cups sifted cake flour
½ cup cocoa

1 teaspoon baking
   powder
1 teaspoon soda
Dash of salt
¾ cup cold water
Chocolate "Philly"
   Frosting

Combine salad dressing and sugar. Blend in vanilla. Add sifted dry ingredients to salad dressing mixture alternately with water, mixing well after each addition. Pour into two greased and floured 8-inch layer pans. Bake at 350°, 25 to 30 minutes. Cool 10 minutes; remove from pans. Frost with:

Chocolate "Philly" Frosting: Combine one 8-oz. pkg. Philadelphia Brand cream cheese, softened, 1 tablespoon milk, 1 teaspoon vanilla and dash of salt. Mix until well blended. Gradually add 5 cups sifted confectioners' sugar. Stir in three 1-oz. squares unsweetened chocolate, melted.

"Philly" Christmas Cake

A glamorous Kraft "classic" for holiday entertaining.

1 8-oz. pkg. Philadelphia
   Brand cream cheese
1 cup margarine
1½ cups sugar
1½ teaspoons vanilla
4 eggs
2¼ cups sifted cake flour

1½ teaspoons baking
   powder
1 cup mixed diced
   candied fruit
½ cup chopped pecans
   *   *   *
½ cup finely chopped
   pecans

Combine softened cream cheese, margarine, sugar and vanilla, mixing until well blended. Add eggs, one at a time, mixing well after each addition. Gradually add 2 cups flour sifted with baking powder; mix well. Combine fruit and chopped nuts with remaining flour; fold into batter.

Grease 10-inch Bundt or tube pan; sprinkle with finely chopped nuts. Pour batter into pan. Bake at 325°, 1 hour and 20 minutes. Cool 5 minutes; remove from pan.

Yuletide Fruitcake

This updated version of an old favorite makes a gracious gift.

3¼ cups flour
1 cup sugar
1½ teaspoons soda
1 teaspoon salt
3 eggs, beaten
¾ cup Squeeze Parkay
  margarine
2 teaspoons vanilla

2 cups ready-to-use
  mincemeat
1⅔ cups mixed diced
  candied fruit
1½ cups chopped pecans
¾ cup chopped dates
Apple jelly

Combine 2½ cups flour, sugar, soda and salt. Add eggs, margarine and vanilla; mix well. Combine remaining flour, mincemeat, candied fruit, nuts and dates; fold into batter. Pour into greased and floured 10-inch tube pan. Bake at 300°, 2 hours. Cool 10 minutes; remove from pan. Glaze with heated jelly.

Variation: Prepare recipe as directed, except for baking. Spoon batter into greased miniature muffin pans, filling each cup ⅔ full. Bake at 300°, 25 minutes.

Creamy Mallow Cheesecake

An easy no-bake dessert—marshmallows are the secret.

1 cup vanilla wafer
  crumbs
¼ cup margarine, melted
    * * *
4 cups Kraft miniature
  marshmallows
⅓ cup milk
2 8-oz. pkgs. cream
  cheese

2 tablespoons lemon
  juice
2 tablespoons grated
  lemon rind
1 teaspoon vanilla
1 cup heavy cream,
  whipped

Combine crumbs and margarine; reserve ¼ cup. Press remaining crumbs onto bottom of 9-inch springform pan.

Melt marshmallows with milk in saucepan over low heat; stir occasionally until smooth. Chill until slightly thickened; mix until well blended. Combine softened cream cheese, lemon juice, rind and vanilla, mixing at medium speed on electric mixer until well blended. Beat in marshmallow mixture; fold in whipped cream. Pour over crust; sprinkle with reserved crumbs. Chill.

Hollywood Cheesecake

1 cup graham cracker
  crumbs
3 tablespoons sugar
3 tablespoons margarine,
  melted

* * *

2 8-oz. pkgs. Philadelphia
  Brand cream cheese
½ cup sugar

1 tablespoon lemon juice
1 teaspoon grated lemon
  rind
½ teaspoon vanilla
2 eggs, separated

* * *

1 cup dairy sour cream
2 tablespoons sugar
1 teaspoon vanilla

Combine crumbs, sugar and margarine; press onto bottom of 9-inch springform pan. Bake at 325°, 10 minutes.

Combine softened cream cheese, sugar, lemon juice, rind and vanilla, mixing at medium speed on electric mixer until well blended. Add egg yolks, one at a time, mixing well after each addition. Fold in stiffly beaten egg whites; pour over crust. Bake at 300°, 45 minutes.

Combine sour cream, sugar and vanilla. Carefully spread over cheesecake; continue baking 10 minutes. Loosen cake from rim of pan; cool before removing rim of pan. Chill.

Kasekuchen

⅓ cup margarine
⅓ cup sugar
1 egg
1¼ cups flour

* * *

3 8-oz. pkgs. cream
  cheese

¾ cup sugar
2 tablespoons flour
1 teaspoon vanilla
3 eggs
2 tablespoons milk
1 10-oz. jar Kraft
  strawberry preserves

Cream margarine and sugar. Blend in egg. Add flour; mix well. Spread on bottom and 1½ inches high around sides of 9-inch springform pan. Bake at 450°, 5 minutes.

Combine softened cream cheese, sugar, flour and vanilla, mixing at medium speed on electric mixer until well blended. Add eggs, one at a time, mixing well after each addition; stir in milk. Pour into pastry-lined pan; bake at 450°, 10 minutes. Reduce heat to 250°; continue baking 25 minutes. Loosen cake from rim of pan; cool before removing rim of pan. Chill. Spread with preserves.

Supreme Cheesecake

Cheesecakes have been a Kraft specialty since "Philly" cream cheese was first marketed in the 1920s. This high, delicate-textured cheesecake was a Kraft original and is still popular today.

1 cup graham cracker crumbs	½ cup sugar
3 tablespoons sugar	2 tablespoons flour
3 tablespoons margarine, melted	¼ teaspoon salt
* * *	4 eggs, separated
2 8-oz. pkgs. Philadelphia Brand cream cheese	⅔ cup half and half
	1 teaspoon vanilla

Combine crumbs, sugar and margarine; press onto bottom of 9-inch springform pan. Bake at 325°, 10 minutes.

Combine softened cream cheese, sugar, flour and salt, mixing at medium speed on electric mixer until well blended. Add egg yolks, one at a time, mixing well after each addition. Blend in half and half and vanilla. Fold in stiffly beaten egg whites; pour over crust. Bake at 325°, 1 hour. Loosen cake from rim of pan; cool before removing rim of pan. Chill.

Crackle-Top Peanut Butter Cookies

An old-fashioned favorite—the sugar coating makes the surface "crackle" while the cookies are baking.

¾ cup Parkay margarine	1 egg
Granulated sugar	1 teaspoon vanilla
¾ cup packed brown sugar	1¾ cups flour
¾ cup creamy peanut butter	½ teaspoon soda
	½ teaspoon salt

Cream margarine, ¾ cup granulated sugar and brown sugar until light and fluffy. Blend in peanut butter, egg and vanilla. Add combined dry ingredients; mix well. Shape rounded teaspoonfuls of dough into balls; roll in granulated sugar. Place on ungreased cookie sheet. Bake at 375°, 10 to 12 minutes. Approximately 4 dozen

Date Nut Jumbos

This tasty, hearty cookie makes a great after-school snack for hungry students.

½ cup Parkay margarine
¾ cup packed brown
   sugar
1 egg
1 teaspoon vanilla
1¼ cups flour
½ teaspoon baking
   powder

½ teaspoon soda
½ teaspoon salt
2 cups corn flakes
1 cup chopped pitted
   dates
½ cup chopped walnuts

Cream margarine and sugar until light and fluffy. Blend in egg and vanilla. Add combined flour, baking powder, soda and salt; mix well. Stir in remaining ingredients. Chill. Shape dough into 1-inch balls; place on ungreased cookie sheet. Bake at 375°, 10 to 12 minutes. Approximately 3½ dozen

Variation: Substitute raisins for dates.

Fruit Kolacky

Sometimes spelled "kolache," these delectable jam-filled cookies are a traditional European specialty. This Kraft version is made with flaky cream cheese pastry.

1 cup margarine
1 8-oz. pkg. cream cheese
2 tablespoons sugar
2¼ cups flour
2 teaspoons baking
   powder

¼ teaspoon salt
Kraft strawberry, red
   raspberry and apricot
   preserves

Combine margarine, softened cream cheese and sugar, mixing until well blended. Add combined dry ingredients; mix well. Knead ten to fifteen times to form stiff dough; chill. On lightly floured surface, roll out dough to ¼-inch thickness; cut with assorted 2-inch cookie cutters. Place on ungreased cookie sheet. Indent centers; fill with preserves. Bake at 350°, 15 to 18 minutes. Sprinkle lightly with confectioners' sugar, if desired. Approximately 5 dozen

Pecan Petites

Crisp, rich and nutty, these sugar-coated party cookies often appear at showers, weddings and holiday buffets. They're a tradition at Christmas.

1 cup Parkay margarine
¼ cup granulated sugar
1 teaspoon vanilla

2 cups flour
1 cup chopped pecans
Confectioners' sugar

Cream margarine and granulated sugar until light and fluffy. Blend in vanilla. Add flour; mix well. Stir in nuts. Shape rounded teaspoonfuls of dough into balls; place on ungreased cookie sheet. Bake at 325°, 20 minutes. Cool slightly; roll in confectioners' sugar. Approximately 3 dozen

Brown-Eyed Susans

A rich, chocolate-topped cookie with almond "eyes"—the popularity of this Kraft "classic" dates from the 1940s and has not diminished with passing time.

1 cup Parkay margarine
¼ cup sugar
½ teaspoon almond
    extract

2 cups flour
½ teaspoon salt
Chocolate Frosting
Whole almonds

Cream margarine and sugar until light and fluffy. Blend in extract. Add flour and salt; mix well. Shape rounded teaspoonfuls of dough into balls. Place on ungreased cookie sheet; flatten slightly. Bake at 375°, 10 to 12 minutes. Cool. Frost with Chocolate Frosting; top with almonds. Approximately 5 dozen

Chocolate Frosting: Combine 1 cup sifted confectioners' sugar and 2 tablespoons cocoa. Add 1 tablespoon hot water and ½ teaspoon vanilla; mix well.

Kraft initiated "open dating" for all Kraft branded products in 1973. The "freshness" date indicates that the product is "best when purchased by (day, month, year)." This date assures peak flavor and freshness at the time of purchase and for a reasonable period when kept under accepted home storage conditions.

Pecan Petites, Brown-Eyed Susans and Sesame Cookies (recipe, page 192)→

Sesame Cookies *(Illustrated page 191)*

Also known as "benne wafers" or "thumb prints," these cookies can be topped with any preserve.

1 cup Parkay margarine	2 cups flour
¼ cup sugar	½ teaspoon salt
1 teaspoon almond	Sesame seeds
extract	Strawberry preserves

Cream margarine and sugar until light and fluffy. Blend in extract. Add flour and salt; mix well. Shape rounded tablespoonfuls of dough into balls; roll in sesame seeds. Place on ungreased cookie sheet. Indent centers; fill with preserves. Bake at 400°, 10 to 12 minutes. Approximately 3 dozen

Variation: Substitute chopped pecans for sesame seeds.

Crunchies

A favorite treat for children, these cookies are crisp and crunchy—and economical!

½ cup Parkay margarine	1¼ cups flour
¾ cup packed brown	½ teaspoon baking
sugar	powder
1 egg	¼ teaspoon salt
1 teaspoon vanilla	2 cups crisp rice cereal

Cream margarine and sugar until light and fluffy. Blend in egg and vanilla. Add combined flour, baking powder and salt; mix well. Stir in cereal. Drop rounded teaspoonfuls of dough onto greased cookie sheet. Bake at 375°, 8 to 10 minutes. Approximately 3½ dozen

"Philly" Sprites

A cream cheese version of spritz and a Kraft "classic."

1 cup margarine	1 teaspoon vanilla
1 8-oz. pkg. Philadelphia	2 cups flour
Brand cream cheese	Dash of salt
⅔ cup sugar	

Combine margarine, softened cream cheese and sugar, mixing until well blended. Blend in vanilla. Add flour and salt; mix well. Chill. Force dough through cookie press onto ungreased cookie sheet. Bake at 400°, 8 to 10 minutes. Approximately 8 dozen

Spicy Thins

These crisp, spicy wafers are traditional Swedish Christmas cookies that can be made in advance and frozen until the holidays.

1 cup Parkay margarine	3 cups flour
1½ cups sugar	2 teaspoons soda
1 egg	2 teaspoons cinnamon
2 tablespoons dark corn syrup	2 teaspoons ginger
	2 teaspoons cloves

Cream margarine and sugar until light and fluffy. Blend in egg and corn syrup. Add combined dry ingredients; mix well. Chill. On lightly floured surface, roll out dough to ⅛-inch thickness; cut with assorted 3-inch cookie cutters. Place on greased cookie sheet. Bake at 400°, 6 to 8 minutes. Approximately 6½ dozen

Swiss Chocolate Squares

A top request item and a particular favorite with the Kraft Kitchens' staff. Made to order for teen get-togethers.

1 cup water	* * *
½ cup Parkay margarine	½ cup Parkay margarine
1½ 1-oz. squares unsweetened chocolate	6 tablespoons milk
2 cups flour	1½ 1-oz. squares unsweetened chocolate
2 cups sugar	4½ cups sifted confectioners' sugar
2 eggs	1 teaspoon vanilla
½ cup dairy sour cream	½ cup chopped nuts
1 teaspoon soda	
½ teaspoon salt	

Combine water, margarine and chocolate in saucepan; bring to boil. Remove from heat. Stir in combined flour and sugar. Add eggs, sour cream, soda and salt; mix well. Pour into greased and floured 15½ × 10½-inch jelly roll pan. Bake at 375°, 20 to 25 minutes.

Combine margarine, milk and chocolate in saucepan; bring to boil. Remove from heat. Add sugar; beat until smooth. Stir in vanilla. Frost cake while warm; sprinkle with nuts. Cool; cut into squares.

Fantasy Fudge

It's almost impossible to fail with this creamy textured fudge —you don't even need a candy thermometer or detailed instructions for success.

3 cups sugar
¾ cup margarine
⅔ cup (5⅓-fl. oz. can) evaporated milk
1 12-oz. pkg. semi-sweet chocolate pieces

1 7-oz. jar Kraft marshmallow creme
1 cup chopped nuts
1 teaspoon vanilla

Combine sugar, margarine and milk in heavy saucepan; bring to full rolling boil, stirring constantly. Continue boiling 5 minutes over medium heat, stirring constantly. (Mixture scorches easily.) Remove from heat; stir in chocolate until melted. Add marshmallow creme, nuts and vanilla; beat until well blended. Pour into greased 13×9-inch baking pan. Cool at room temperature; cut into squares. 3 pounds

Variation: Substitute 1 cup creamy or chunk style peanut butter for chocolate pieces; omit nuts.

Caramel Apples

Americans have been dipping and munching caramel apples since these famous caramels were introduced in the mid-1930s.

49 (14-oz. bag) Kraft caramels
2 tablespoons water

4 or 5 medium size apples, washed, dried
Wooden sticks

Melt caramels with water in covered double boiler or in saucepan over low heat. Stir occasionally until sauce is smooth. Insert a wooden stick into stem end of each apple. Dip into hot caramel sauce; turn until coated. Scrape off excess sauce from bottom of apples. Place on greased waxed paper; chill until firm. Keep in cool place.

Variations: Dip Caramel Apples in shredded coconut or chopped nuts. Substitute pears for apples.

A recent innovation and a definite convenience are Wrapples caramel sheets. Simply wrap an apple with a caramel sheet and heat for 5 minutes in a 200° oven.

Crispy Confections

Quick and delicious—an all-time Kraft favorite.

49 (14-oz. bag) Kraft
    caramels
3 tablespoons water
2 cups crisp rice cereal

2 cups corn flakes
1 4-oz. pkg. shredded
    coconut

Melt caramels with water in saucepan over low heat. Stir frequently until sauce is smooth. Pour over combined cereals and coconut; toss until well coated. Drop rounded table-spoonfuls onto greased cookie sheet; let stand until firm. 4 dozen

Marshmallow Crispy Treats

A longtime favorite with children. This mildly sweet, crispy confection is made with only three ingredients.

¼ cup margarine
4 cups Kraft miniature
    marshmallows

5 cups crisp rice cereal

Melt margarine in 3-quart saucepan over low heat. Add marshmallows; stir occasionally until smooth. Remove from heat. Stir in cereal until well coated; press into greased 13 × 9-inch pan. Cool; cut into squares.

Chocolate "Philly" Fudge

When "Philly" Fudge was first demonstrated on television in 1951, over a million viewers requested the recipe.

4 cups sifted
    confectioners' sugar
1 8-oz. pkg. Philadelphia
    Brand cream cheese
4 1-oz. squares
    unsweetened
    chocolate, melted

1 teaspoon vanilla
Dash of salt
½ cup chopped nuts

Gradually add sugar to softened cream cheese, mixing until well blended. Stir in remaining ingredients. Spread in greased 8-inch square pan. Chill several hours or overnight. 1¾ pounds

Alaska Pie

An elegant dessert to impress discriminating guests.

1½ cups graham cracker crumbs	1 qt. ice cream, softened
3 tablespoons sugar	3 egg whites
6 tablespoons margarine, melted	Dash of salt
	1 cup Kraft marshmallow creme

* * *

Combine crumbs, sugar and margarine; press onto bottom and sides of 9-inch pie plate. Bake at 375°, 8 minutes. Cool.

Fill crust with softened ice cream. Freeze. Beat egg whites and salt until soft peaks form. Gradually add marshmallow creme, beating until stiff peaks form. Spread over frozen ice cream pie, sealing to edge of crust. Bake at 500°, 3 minutes or until lightly browned. Serve immediately.

To Make Ahead: Prepare recipe as directed, except for final baking. Freeze several hours or overnight. When ready to serve, bake as directed.

Almost any ice cream is delicious in this meringue-topped pie. Try fresh peach or strawberry, chocolate, fudge-nut or New York cherry.

Strawberry Cream Cheese Pie

A glorious strawberry pie with a marvelous cream cheese layer!

1 8-oz. pkg. Philadelphia Brand cream cheese	2 pts. whole strawberries
2 tablespoons milk	½ cup sugar
2 tablespoons sugar	2 tablespoons cornstarch
1 9-inch baked pastry shell	⅓ cup water

Combine softened cream cheese, milk and sugar, mixing until well blended. Spread onto bottom of pastry shell; cover with 1 pint strawberries. Combine sugar and cornstarch in saucepan; gradually add water. Bring to boil, stirring constantly. Cook 1 minute or until mixture is clear and thickened. Halve remaining strawberries; add to cornstarch mixture. Pour over whole strawberries. Chill several hours or overnight.

Cheddar-Crust Apple Pie

Apples and cheese are natural companions. This golden cheddar crust is something special for the spicy apple filling.

1½ cups flour
Dash of salt
½ cup shortening
1½ cups (6 ozs.) shredded
Kraft sharp cheddar
cheese
4 to 6 tablespoons water

* * *

½ cup sugar
2 tablespoons flour
¼ teaspoon cinnamon
6 cups peeled apple
slices
2 tablespoons margarine

Combine flour and salt; cut in shortening until mixture resembles coarse crumbs. Stir in cheese. Sprinkle with water while mixing lightly with a fork; form into ball. Divide dough in half. On lightly floured surface, roll one half to 12-inch circle. Place in 9-inch pie plate.

Combine sugar, flour and cinnamon; toss with apples. Place in pastry shell; dot with margarine. Roll out remaining dough to 12-inch circle; place over apple mixture. Seal and flute edges of pastry; cut slits in top. Bake at 425°, 35 minutes.

Pineapple "Philly" Pie

One of many delicious Kraft cream cheese pies—this one has a clear pineapple filling topped with a cream cheese custard.

⅓ cup sugar
1 tablespoon cornstarch
1 8¼-oz. can crushed
pineapple, undrained
1 9-inch unbaked pastry
shell

* * *

1 8-oz. pkg. Philadelphia
Brand cream cheese
½ cup sugar
½ teaspoon salt
2 eggs
½ cup milk
½ teaspoon vanilla
¼ cup chopped pecans

Combine sugar and cornstarch in saucepan; gradually add pineapple. Cook, stirring constantly, until clear and thickened. Cool; spread on bottom of pastry shell.

Combine softened cream cheese, sugar and salt, mixing until well blended. Add eggs, one at a time, mixing well after each addition. Blend in milk and vanilla. Pour over pineapple mixture; sprinkle with nuts. Bake at 400°, 15 minutes. Reduce temperature to 325°; continue baking 40 minutes. Cool.

Caramel Pecan Pie

This is a caramel version of a southwestern specialty—enjoy it, and don't count the calories!

36 Kraft caramels	½ teaspoon vanilla
¼ cup water	¼ teaspoon salt
¼ cup margarine	1 cup pecan halves
¾ cup sugar	1 9-inch unbaked pastry
3 eggs, beaten	shell

Melt caramels with water and margarine in saucepan over low heat. Stir frequently until sauce is smooth. Combine sugar, eggs, vanilla and salt. Gradually add caramel sauce; mix well. Stir in nuts; pour into pastry shell. Bake at 350°, 45 to 50 minutes. Pie filling will appear to be very soft, but becomes firm as it cools.

Tahiti Cream Pie

A taste of the tropics in this cool, fluffy mallow pie.

1½ cups graham cracker crumbs	1 8¼-oz. can crushed pineapple, drained
3 tablespoons sugar	1 3½-oz. can flaked coconut
6 tablespoons margarine, melted	2 cups Kraft miniature marshmallows
* * *	1 cup heavy cream, whipped
1 3⅛-oz. pkg. vanilla pudding and pie filling mix	

Combine crumbs, sugar and margarine; press onto bottom and sides of 9-inch pie plate. Bake at 375°, 8 minutes. Cool.

Prepare mix as directed for pie filling on package, except using 1½ cups milk. Add pineapple and ¾ cup coconut. Cover surface of pie filling with waxed paper or transparent wrap; chill. Mix until well blended; fold in marshmallows and whipped cream. Pour into crumb crust; sprinkle with remaining coconut. Chill several hours or overnight.

Nutrition labels appear on all Kraft branded products which in normal consumption make a significant nutritional contribution to the total diet, or which fill a special dietary need.

Banana Mallow Party Pie

A Kraft original that has appeared repeatedly on television commercials and in magazine ads.

1 3⅛-oz. pkg. vanilla
    pudding and pie
    filling mix
1½ cups Kraft miniature
    marshmallows

1 cup heavy cream,
    whipped
2 bananas
1 9-inch baked vanilla
    wafer crust, chilled

Prepare mix as directed for pie filling on package, except using 1¾ cups milk. Cover surface of pie filling with waxed paper or transparent wrap; chill. Mix until well blended; fold in marshmallows and whipped cream. Slice bananas into crust. Pour filling over bananas. Chill several hours or overnight.

Paradise Pumpkin Pie

This festive pie has a unique cream cheese layer that blends beautifully with the spicy filling.

1 8-oz. pkg. Philadelphia
    Brand cream cheese
¼ cup sugar
½ teaspoon vanilla
1 egg
1 9-inch unbaked pastry
    shell

* * *

1¼ cups canned pumpkin

1 cup evaporated milk
½ cup sugar
2 eggs, slightly beaten
1 teaspoon cinnamon
¼ teaspoon ginger
¼ teaspoon nutmeg
    Dash of salt
    Maple syrup

Combine softened cream cheese, sugar and vanilla, mixing until well blended. Add egg; mix well. Spread onto bottom of pastry shell.

Combine remaining ingredients except syrup; mix well. Carefully pour over cream cheese mixture. Bake at 350°, 1 hour and 5 minutes. Cool. Brush with syrup.

Kraft has always guaranteed complete product satisfaction. To emphasize this policy, this statement appears on every Kraft branded product: "Satisfaction guaranteed or your money back from Kraft."

Banana Mallow Party Pie→

"Philly" Pastry

A delicate, flaky crust with the unique "Philly" cream cheese flavor—it's delicious for fruit or cream pies, or for quiches.

> 1 3-oz. pkg. Philadelphia
>   Brand cream cheese
> ⅓ cup margarine
>
> 1 cup flour
> ⅛ teaspoon salt

Combine softened cream cheese and margarine, mixing until well blended. Add flour and salt; mix well. Form into ball; chill thoroughly. On lightly floured surface, roll out dough to 12-inch circle. Place in 9-inch pie plate. Trim and flute edge; prick bottom and sides with fork. Bake at 400°, 15 minutes or until golden brown. One 9-inch pastry shell

Variation: For tart shells, divide dough into 24 balls; press into miniature muffin pan. Bake at 400°, 10 to 12 minutes.

For pies that bake longer than 40 minutes, cover rim of pie with aluminum foil to prevent excess browning.

Crisp Crust Pastry

Tender and flaky—golden crust for any favorite filling, sweet or savory.

> 2 cups flour
> ½ teaspoon salt
> ⅔ cup Parkay margarine
>
> 4 to 6 tablespoons cold
>   water

Combine flour and salt; cut in margarine until mixture resembles coarse crumbs. Sprinkle with water while mixing lightly with a fork; form into ball. Divide dough in half. On lightly floured surface, roll out each half to 12-inch circle. Place in 9-inch pie plates. Trim and flute edges; prick bottoms and sides with fork. Two 9-inch pastry shells

For fillings that don't require baking, bake the crust at 450°, 10 minutes.

In 1973, Kraft adopted Universal Product Code (UPC) labeling—an industry-wide system of identifying individual products with a 10-digit symbol which can be read by an electronic scanner. The system provides benefits in efficiency, accuracy, and cost savings for the retailer and consumer.

Chocolate "Philly" Soufflé

2 tablespoons margarine
2 tablespoons flour
½ cup milk
½ teaspoon salt
1 8-oz. pkg. Philadelphia
   Brand cream cheese,
   cubed

⅔ cup sugar
2 1-oz. squares
   unsweetened
   chocolate, melted
1½ teaspoons vanilla
4 eggs, separated

Make a white sauce with margarine, flour, milk and salt. Add cream cheese, ⅓ cup sugar, chocolate and vanilla; stir over low heat until smooth. Remove from heat. Gradually add slightly beaten egg yolks; cool slightly. Beat egg whites until soft peaks form. Gradually add remaining sugar, beating until stiff peaks form. Fold cream cheese mixture into egg whites. Pour into 1¼-quart soufflé dish or casserole. Bake at 350°, 1 hour. Serve immediately. 6 servings

Caramel Praline Soufflé

1 envelope unflavored
   gelatin
1½ cups cold water
28 Kraft caramels
2 tablespoons sugar
5 eggs, separated

1 cup heavy cream,
   whipped
* * *
2 tablespoons sugar
¼ cup chopped pecans,
   toasted

Combine gelatin and ½ cup cold water. Melt caramels and sugar with remaining water in saucepan over low heat. Stir frequently until sauce is smooth. Stir small amount of hot mixture into egg yolks; return to hot mixture. Cook 3 to 5 minutes over low heat, stirring constantly, until thickened. Stir in gelatin. Cool to room temperature. Fold stiffly beaten egg whites and whipped cream into caramel mixture.

Wrap a 3-inch collar of aluminum foil around top of 1-quart soufflé dish; secure with tape. Pour mixture into dish; chill until firm. Remove foil collar before serving.

Melt sugar in skillet over medium heat until clear and caramel colored. Stir in nuts; spoon onto greased cookie sheet. Immediately separate nuts with two forks. Cool; break into small pieces. Sprinkle over soufflé before serving. 6 servings

Strawberry Romanoff Soufflé

Chilled soufflés look gorgeous, can be made in advance, and never fail—great advantages for entertaining with ease.

1 envelope unflavored
    gelatin
¼ cup cold water
1 8-oz. pkg. cream cheese
1 10-oz. pkg. frozen
    strawberries, thawed

¼ cup Cointreau liqueur
2 egg whites
1 7-oz. jar Kraft
    marshmallow creme
1 cup heavy cream,
    whipped

Combine gelatin and water in saucepan; let stand 1 minute. Stir over medium heat until dissolved. Gradually add to softened cream cheese, mixing until well blended. Stir in strawberries and liqueur; chill until slightly thickened. Beat egg whites until soft peaks form. Gradually add marshmallow creme, beating until stiff peaks form. Fold egg white mixture and whipped cream into gelatin mixture.

Wrap a 3-inch collar of aluminum foil around top of 1-quart soufflé dish; secure with tape. Pour mixture into dish; chill until firm. Remove foil collar before serving. 8 to 10 servings

Variation: Frozen raspberries can be substituted for strawberries.

Dessert Cheese Tray

Dessert cheese and fruit trays are colorful, attractive and compatible with almost any menu from casual to elegant— in pairing fruit and cheese, be guided by your own creativity and personal preferences.

Swiss cheese, cut into
    cubes
Cracker Barrel sharp
    cheddar cheese, sliced
Blue cheese

Tiny Dane Danish
    camembert cheese
Edam cheese
Grapes

Arrange cheese and fruit on serving tray as desired.

Cheese is available in so many sizes, shapes, flavors and textures that the possibilities for imaginative cheese arrangements are almost unlimited. In addition, there is a wide selection of fruit—apples, pears, grapes, melon, peaches, figs, dates—to complement cheese.

Apple Crisp

A traditional autumn dessert—serve it warm, topped with shredded cheddar cheese or whipped cream cheese.

6 cups peeled apple
  slices
¼ cup water
1 cup flour
¾ cup packed brown
  sugar

1 teaspoon cinnamon
½ teaspoon salt
½ cup Parkay margarine

Place apples and water in 10 × 6-inch baking dish. Combine dry ingredients; cut in margarine until mixture resembles coarse crumbs. Sprinkle over apples. Bake at 350°, 40 minutes or until apples are tender. 6 servings

This spicy apple dessert can be made with almost any type of apple that has a firm, crisp texture and a tart flavor— Winesap, Jonathan and Rome Beauty are good choices.

Bavarian Cream

This simplified Bavarian cream, a Kraft "classic," is made with cream cheese and is delicious served with fresh berries or sliced peaches.

1 envelope unflavored
  gelatin
¼ cup cold water
1 8-oz. pkg. Philadelphia
  Brand cream cheese
½ cup sugar
½ teaspoon almond
  extract

Dash of salt
1 cup milk
1 cup heavy cream,
  whipped
1 pt. whole strawberries

Combine gelatin and cold water in saucepan; let stand 1 minute. Stir over medium heat until dissolved. Combine softened cream cheese, sugar, extract and salt, mixing until well blended. Gradually add gelatin and milk. Chill until slightly thickened. Mix until well blended; fold in whipped cream. Pour into 1½-quart mold; chill until firm. Unmold; serve with strawberries. 8 servings

This dessert can also be prepared in individual molds.

Chantilly Creme Crepes

These banana cream crepes (a particular favorite with the television photography crew) are a wonderful special occasion or company dessert.

3 eggs, beaten
⅔ cup flour
½ teaspoon salt
1 cup milk
     * * *
1 7-oz. jar Kraft
   marshmallow creme
2 tablespoons orange
   juice

¼ teaspoon grated orange
   rind
1 cup heavy cream,
   whipped
2 bananas, sliced
   Slivered almonds,
   toasted

Combine eggs, flour, salt and milk; beat until smooth. Let stand 30 minutes. For each crepe, pour ¼ cup batter into hot, lightly greased 8-inch skillet or crepe pan. Cook on one side only.

Combine marshmallow creme, orange juice and rind; mix until well blended. Fold in whipped cream. Fill each crepe with banana slices and ¼ cup creme mixture; roll up. Top with remaining creme mixture and nuts. 8 servings

The crepes can be prepared in advance, stacked, wrapped and frozen.

Curried Fruit Compote

Sweetened with brown sugar, mildly flavored with curry, this compote is attractive and delicious for buffet dining.

1 20-oz. can pineapple
   chunks, drained
1 17-oz. can pitted dark
   sweet cherries, drained
1 16-oz. can apricot
   halves, drained

¼ cup packed brown
   sugar
1 teaspoon curry powder
¼ cup margarine
   Philadelphia Brand
   Whipped cream
   cheese

Place combined fruit in 1-quart casserole. Sprinkle with sugar and curry powder; dot with margarine. Bake at 350°, 20 minutes. Spoon into dessert dishes; top with cream cheese. 6 to 8 servings

Chelsea Trifle

A superb adaptation of an elegant English dessert! Trifle is traditionally served in a clear glass or cut crystal bowl.

3 cups Kraft miniature
   marshmallows
¾ cup milk
2 eggs, beaten
2 tablespoons brandy
1 cup heavy cream,
   whipped

8 to 10 thin jelly roll
   slices
1 16-oz. can apricot
   halves, drained

Melt marshmallows with milk in saucepan over low heat; stir occasionally until smooth. Add small amount of hot mixture to eggs; return to hot mixture. Cook 2 to 3 minutes over low heat, stirring constantly, until thickened. Remove from heat; add brandy. Chill until slightly thickened. Mix until well blended; fold in whipped cream. Line 1½-quart bowl with jelly roll slices and apricots; fill with marshmallow mixture. Chill several hours or overnight. 8 to 10 servings

Variation: 2 cups raspberries, strawberry or peach slices can be substituted for apricots.

Grasshopper Torte

A do-ahead frozen dessert that offers elegance with ease, this Kraft "classic" is often served at luncheons in the Kitchens' dining room.

2 cups (24) crushed
   cream-filled chocolate
   cookies
¼ cup margarine, melted
   *   *   *

1 7-oz. jar Kraft
   marshmallow creme
¼ cup creme de menthe
2 cups heavy cream,
   whipped

Combine crumbs and margarine; reserve ½ cup. Press remaining crumbs onto bottom of 9-inch springform pan. Chill.

Combine marshmallow creme and creme de menthe; mix until well blended. Fold in whipped cream. Pour into pan; sprinkle with reserved crumbs. Freeze.

Variation: Prepare the torte in a 9-inch pie plate.

Dutch Boy Pancake

A German specialty, this impressive puffy pancake resembles a huge popover—a delightful dessert to serve late evening guests.

1 7-oz. jar Kraft
   marshmallow creme
1 8-oz. pkg. cream cheese
   * * *
2 eggs
½ cup flour

¼ teaspoon salt
½ cup milk
1 tablespoon margarine
1 qt. sliced strawberries,
   sliced peaches or
   blueberries

Gradually add marshmallow creme to softened cream cheese, mixing until well blended.

Combine eggs, flour, salt and milk; beat until smooth. Heat heavy oven-proof 9-inch skillet in 450° oven until very hot. Coat skillet with margarine; immediately add batter. Bake on lowest shelf in oven at 450°, 10 minutes. Reduce heat to 350°; continue baking 10 minutes or until golden brown. Fill with fruit; top with cream cheese mixture. Serve immediately. 6 to 8 servings

Saucy Lemon Pudding

An old-fashioned favorite, this pudding separates as it bakes into a delicate sponge layer and a creamy lemon sauce.

⅓ cup Parkay margarine
1 cup sugar
2 eggs, separated
2 tablespoons lemon
   juice

1 tablespoon grated
   lemon rind
⅓ cup flour
1 cup milk

Cream margarine and ¾ cup sugar until light and fluffy. Blend in egg yolks, lemon juice and rind. Add flour; mix well. Stir in milk. Beat egg whites until soft peaks form. Gradually add remaining sugar, beating until stiff peaks form. Fold into batter; pour into eight 6-oz. custard cups. Set custard cups in baking pan; pour in boiling water to ½-inch depth. Bake at 350°, 35 to 40 minutes. Remove from water; cool 10 minutes. Invert on dessert dishes. 8 servings

Variation: Prepare recipe as directed. Pour batter into 1-quart casserole. Bake at 350°, 40 to 45 minutes. Cool 20 minutes; invert on serving plate.

Heavenly Hash

A combination of rice, fruit, marshmallows and cream, this traditional Swedish dessert has become a Kraft television favorite.

2 cups Kraft miniature
    marshmallows
2 cups cooked rice,
    chilled
1 8¼-oz. can crushed
    pineapple, drained
½ cup maraschino cherry
    halves

¼ cup slivered almonds,
    toasted
1 cup heavy cream
¼ cup sugar
1 teaspoon vanilla

Combine marshmallows, rice, fruit and nuts. Whip cream, gradually adding sugar and vanilla; fold into rice mixture. Chill. 8 servings

Pot de Creme

A Kraft version of a French specialty—marshmallows are the secret of the smooth richness, chocolate and brandy of the appealing flavor combination.

4 cups Kraft miniature
    marshmallows
¼ cup milk
1 1-oz. square
    unsweetened
    chocolate

2 eggs, beaten
1 teaspoon brandy
    flavoring
1 cup heavy cream,
    whipped

Melt marshmallows with milk and chocolate in saucepan over low heat; stir occasionally until smooth. Add small amount of hot mixture to eggs; return to hot mixture. Cook 2 to 3 minutes, stirring constantly, until thickened. Remove from heat; add flavoring. Chill until slightly thickened. Mix until well blended; fold in whipped cream. Spoon into six dessert dishes; chill several hours or overnight. 6 servings

Literally translated as "pot of cream," this rich French pudding is traditionally served in tiny, covered pot de creme cups. Stemmed dessert dishes or small wine glasses are attractive substitutes.

Mocha Tortoni

Quick, easy and very creamy! This delicate coffee-nut frozen dessert is an excellent do-ahead for entertaining—double or triple the recipe to fit the crowd.

1 teaspoon instant coffee
1 cup heavy cream
1 cup Kraft marshmallow
    creme

½ cup chopped walnuts
Chocolate topping

Dissolve coffee in heavy cream. Combine marshmallow creme and 2 tablespoons coffee mixture; mix until well blended. Whip remaining coffee mixture until stiff. Fold in marshmallow creme mixture and nuts. Spoon into six dessert dishes or 5-oz. paper cups. Freeze. Place in refrigerator ½ hour before serving. Serve with chocolate topping. 6 servings

Variation: Substitute 1 tablespoon coffee liqueur for instant coffee.

Spanish Flan

A Kraft variation of a Spanish favorite. In this version, a rich caramel sauce replaces the traditional burnt sugar.

14 Kraft caramels
3 tablespoons water
4 eggs
¼ cup sugar

1 teaspoon vanilla
¼ teaspoon salt
2¾ cups milk

Melt caramels with water in saucepan over low heat. Stir frequently until sauce is smooth. Pour into greased 8-inch layer pan. Combine eggs, sugar, vanilla and salt; mix well. Stir in milk. Slowly pour milk mixture over caramel sauce. Set layer pan in baking pan; pour in boiling water to ½-inch depth. Bake at 350°, 40 minutes or until knife inserted in center comes out clean. Remove from water; cool 5 minutes. Invert on serving dish. 6 to 8 servings

The flan is a delicious finale for Mexican or Spanish menus. For a festive dinner, serve "Philly" Avocado Dip, Enchiladas and a tossed salad with the flan.

Strawberries Alexander

Very elegant and very easy—a splendid marshmallow creme variation of the famous Strawberries Romanoff. For a dramatic touch, serve in tall stemmed dessert or champagne glasses.

1 7-oz. jar Kraft
    marshmallow creme
3 tablespoons brandy

1 cup heavy cream,
    whipped
1 qt. whole strawberries

Combine marshmallow creme and brandy; mix until well blended. Fold in whipped cream. Chill. Serve over fruit. 6 servings

Variation: Substitute 1 tablespoon kirsch for brandy.

The fluffy marshmallow creme sauce is delicious on many fruit combinations or baked dessert soufflés.

Strawberry Tiffany Torte

Refreshing and luscious, this layered dessert can be prepared in advance.

2½ cups vanilla wafer
    crumbs
⅓ cup margarine, melted
    * * *
1¾ cups milk
1 8-oz. pkg. Philadelphia
    Brand cream cheese

1 3¾-oz. pkg. vanilla
    instant pudding mix
1 teaspoon grated lemon
    rind
2 pts. strawberries, sliced
4 cups whipped topping

Combine crumbs and margarine; reserve ½ cup. Press remaining crumbs onto bottom of 13 × 9-inch baking pan.

Gradually add ½ cup milk to softened cream cheese, mixing until well blended. Add remaining milk, pudding mix and lemon rind; beat slowly 1 minute. Pour over crust; cover with fruit. Spread topping over fruit; top with reserved crumbs. Chill several hours or overnight. 12 to 15 servings

Variations: For a crisp crust, bake at 350°, 8 minutes. Cool thoroughly before adding filling. Substitute raspberries, blueberries or fresh sliced peaches or nectarines for the strawberries.

Cooking Terms

Baste: Spoon liquid over meat or other foods during cooking to add flavor and prevent drying of the surface. The liquid may be melted fat, meat drippings or sauce.

Beat: Thoroughly combine ingredients and incorporate air with a rapid, regular motion.

Blend: Thoroughly combine two or more ingredients or prepare food in an electric blender.

Boil: Cook in liquid in which bubbles rise continually to the surface and break.

Chill: Refrigerate until cold.

Chop: Cut into pieces of random size.

Coat: Cover surface of food evenly.

Cool: Allow to come to room temperature.

Cream: Soften a fat, such as margarine, by beating with a spoon or mixer. This usually refers to blending a sugar and a fat together.

Cube: Cut into pieces of uniform size and shape, usually ½ inch or larger.

Cut in: Combine solid fat with dry ingredients by using a pastry blender or two knives in a scissor motion until particles are of desired size — i.e., coarse crumbs.

Dash: Add less than ⅛ teaspoon of an ingredient.

Dot: Evenly distribute small amounts of an ingredient such as margarine or preserves.

Fold in: Combine delicate ingredients such as beaten egg whites or whipped cream with other ingredients. Gently cut down through the center of the mixture, across the bottom of the bowl, up and over the top of the mixture, using a circular motion.

Fry: Cook in hot fat.

Grate: Rub on a grater to produce fine pieces.

Grease: Rub fat on surface of pan or dish to prevent sticking.

Heavy Cream: Cream that has a fat content of 30% to 40% and is generally used for whipping.

Knead: Work dough with a press-and-fold motion to evenly distribute ingredients and develop texture. Flatten the ball of dough and fold in half toward you. Press and push away with the heel of your hand. Rotate dough a quarter turn and repeat process until dough surface is smooth.

Marinate: Let stand in a well-seasoned liquid, such as dressing, for a period of time to produce flavor and/or to tenderize.

Mixing just until moistened: Combine ingredients for a batter or dough until dry ingredients are thoroughly moistened, but mixture is still lumpy.

Packed brown sugar: Fill measurer by pressing with a spoon. Sugar will hold its shape when inverted from the measurer.

Partially set: Stage of thickening for gelatin mixture when it is the consistency of unbeaten egg whites.

Rolling boil: Mixture appears to "rise" in the pan. The surface billows rather than just bubbles.

Rounded teaspoon: Measurement for dough, as for cookies, slightly mounded in a flatware (not measuring) teaspoon.

Sauté: Brown or cook in a small amount of hot fat.

Shred: Cut into very thin pieces using a shredder or knife.

Simmer: Cook in liquid just below the boiling point. Bubbles form slowly just below the surface.

Soft peaks: Stage in beating egg whites when mixture will form soft rounded peaks when beaters are removed.

Stiff peaks: Stage in beating egg whites when mixture will hold stiff pointed peaks when beaters are removed. The mixture is glossy, not dry.

Stir-fry: Cook in small amount of fat over medium to high heat, stirring continuously until ingredients are tender, yet crisp.

Toss: Mix lightly with a lifting motion, using two forks or spoons.

Whip: Beat rapidly with a wire whisk, rotary beater, or electric mixer to incorporate air and increase volume.

White Sauce: Basic sauce made with margarine, flour, seasonings and milk. Melt margarine in saucepan over low heat. Blend in flour and seasonings. Gradually add milk; cook, stirring constantly, until thickened.

Substitutions

For	Use
1 teaspoon baking powder	¼ teaspoon baking soda plus ½ teaspoon cream of tartar
1 cup cake flour	1 cup minus 2 tablespoons all purpose flour
1 oz. unsweetened chocolate	3 tablespoons cocoa plus 1 tablespoon fat
1 tablespoon cornstarch	2 tablespoons flour *or* 4 teaspoons quick-cooking tapioca
1 cup light cream	⅞ cup milk plus 3 tablespoons margarine or butter
1 cup heavy cream	¾ cup milk plus ⅓ cup margarine or butter
1 egg	2 egg yolks plus 1 tablespoon water *or* 2 egg yolks (for custard)
1 clove garlic	⅛ teaspoon garlic powder *or* 1 teaspoon garlic salt
1 tablespoon fresh herbs	1 teaspoon dried herbs
1 cup honey	1¼ cups sugar plus ¼ cup liquid
1 cup fresh whole milk	½ cup evaporated milk plus ½ cup water *or* 1 cup reconstituted non-fat dry milk plus 2 teaspoons margarine or butter
1 cup sour milk or buttermilk	1 tablespoon lemon juice or vinegar plus milk to make 1 cup (let stand 5 minutes)
1 lb. fresh mushrooms	6 ozs. canned mushrooms
1 teaspoon dry mustard	1 tablespoon prepared mustard
¼ cup chopped fresh onion	1 tablespoon instant minced onion, rehydrated
1 cake compressed yeast	1 package or 2 teaspoons active dry yeast

Equivalents

Baking Items

Bread Crumbs
Dry	1 cup	= 3 to 4 dried bread slices
Soft	1 cup	= 1½ fresh bread slices
Flour, all purpose	1 lb.	= 4 cups
Gelatin, unflavored	1 envelope	= 1 tablespoon
Graham Cracker Crumbs	1 cup	= 13 square graham crackers, finely crushed

Margarine
Solid Regular	1 stick	= 8 tablespoons
		= ½ cup
		= ¼ lb.
Soft	1 container	= 1 cup
		= ½ lb.
Marshmallows	1 regular marshmallow	= 10 miniature marshmallows
	100 to 110 miniature marshmallows	= 1 cup
Nuts, chopped (peanuts, pecans, walnuts)	4½ ozs.	= 1 cup

Sugar
Brown	1 lb.	= 2¼ cups packed
Confectioners'	1 lb.	= 4½ cups sifted
Granulated	1 lb.	= 2¼ cups

Cheeses

Natural Chunk or Process Cheese	4 ozs.	= 1 cup shredded or cubed
Cottage	1 lb.	= 2 cups
Cream	8 ozs.	= 1 cup

(continued on next page)

Equivalents

Fruits and Vegetables

Apples	3 medium (1 lb.)	= 3 cups sliced
Coconut	3½-oz. can, shredded	= 1⅓ cups
Lemon or Lime	1 medium	= 2 to 3 tablespoons juice = 1 tablespoon grated rind
Onion	1 medium	= ½ cup chopped
Orange	1 medium	= ⅓ to ½ cup juice = 1 to 2 tablespoons grated rind
Potatoes	3 medium (1 lb.)	= 2¼ cups cooked = 1¾ cups mashed

Rice and Pastas

Macaroni, uncooked	4 ozs. (1 cup)	= 2 cups cooked
Noodles, uncooked	4 ozs. (1½ to 2 cups)	= 2 cups cooked
Rice		
Precooked	1 cup	= 2 cups cooked
Uncooked	1 cup	= 3 cups cooked
Spaghetti, uncooked	1 lb.	= 6½ cups cooked

Equivalent Measures

3 teaspoons	= 1 tablespoon
4 tablespoons	= ¼ cup
5⅓ tablespoons	= ⅓ cup
16 tablespoons	= 1 cup
2 cups	= 1 pint
4 quarts	= 1 gallon
8 ozs.	= 1 cup
16 ozs.	= 1 lb.
4 ozs.	= ¼ lb.

Index

221

223